MONTH
OF THE
HOLY SOULS
IN PURGATORY

Prayer book burned by the hand of a soul in Purgatory.
—Chiese del Sacro Cuore del Suffragio,
Rome, Italy

Month of the Holy Souls in Purgatory

OR

PRACTICAL MEDITATIONS FOR EACH DAY OF THE MONTH OF NOVEMBER

BY THE

ABBÉ BERLIOUX

Translated from the French by

Eleanor Cholmeley

MEDIATRIX PRESS
MMXXII

ISBN: 978-1-957066-33-2

Nihil Obstat:
 W. R. WOODS, O.S.B.,
   Censor Deputatus.

Imprimatur:
 ✠HENRICUS EDUARDUS,
   Card Archiepiscopus.

Imprimatur:
 ✠GULIELMUS,
   Archiepiscopus Dublinensis,
     Hiberniæ Primas.
Die 13 *Oct.* 1886.

Cover art: *The Virgin of Carmel and the Souls of Purgatory* —Juan Francisco de Aguilera

Mediatrix Press
607 E 6th Ave
Post Falls, ID 83854
www.mediatrixpress.com

CONTENTS

PREFACE

IN the pride of life the world forgets the Holy Souls in Purgatory. In times of persecution, when death was near, men thought more and had more loving remembrance of the dead. It is to be feared that in these soft days we neither lay to heart as we ought the duty we owe to the Holy Souls, nor keep alive, day by day, the thought how soon we may be likewise in need of the suffrages of the faithful.

This little book will help us to remember them and never to forget our own last end.

HENRY EDWARD,
Card. Archbishop of Westminster

Oct. 13th, 1886.

INTRODUCTION

TO obtain relief for the souls of the faithful departed, and to benefit the living at the same time by so doing, is the two-fold object of this little work. It is well-known in the Christian world, that the prayers of the living are of use to the dead, but what is not sufficiently known is, that the suffrages of the dead themselves are of benefit to the living. Yes, the power and gratitude of the holy souls are too little known and appreciated, and few think of having recourse to their intercession. Nevertheless their influence is so great that we should scarcely believe it, were we not convinced by daily experience.

It is true that the holy souls cannot merit for themselves, this being no longer in their power; but they have the means of making their precious merits of value to us. They can obtain nothing for themselves, but the prayers they offer for us in the midst of their sufferings avail with God. And if they can benefit us so much when in Purgatory, what will they not do for us when they are admitted into heaven! What gratitude will they not feel for their benefactors!

Sts. Liguori, Bellarmine, along with Suarez and most other theologians teach that it is lawful and useful to invoke the souls in Purgatory to obtain the graces and favors we need for soul and body.

St. Teresa used often to say, that everything she asked God, through the intercession of the faithful departed, was granted to her. And we read in the life of St. Catharine of Bologna, that when she wanted very particularly to obtain any grace, she had always recourse to the suffering souls in Purgatory, asking them to present her petitions to God; and invariably her prayer was heard. She, moreover, declared positively that she had very often obtained favors through their intercession that had not been granted to her through the intercession of the saints.

The holy Curé of Ars, when speaking on the subject, said, "if people only knew how great the power of the souls in Purgatory is, and what graces may be obtained through their intercession, they would not be so much forgotten." Oh! let us then pray often for them, so that they may often pray for us.

There are certain temporal favors which seem, more than others, to be granted to the intercession of the holy souls, for instance cures in cases of serious illnesses, preservation from dangers, the gain of a lawsuit, and the success of an important undertaking. God, knowing what importance mankind attaches to these graces of secondary interest, has placed the obtaining of them in the hands of the suffering souls, in order to induce us by this means to obtain assistance for them.

We have, then, everything to gain in this exchange of prayers with the souls of the departed. What an admirable dispensation of Divine Providence, what a consoling article of faith, is that of the Communion of Saints! We by our prayers relieve and deliver the suffering souls from captivity, at the same time they offer to God their prayers, their lamentations, their sufferings, their previous merits, and God bestows upon us the most abundant blessings, both spiritual and temporal.

Stimulated by these advantages, held out to us in return for the faithful observance of the pious practices of this month, let us not fail each day, to visit in spirit, our friends and relatives who may be in Purgatory, as well as the poor souls who are the most abandoned and the most forgotten. Let us bring them some relief – let us hasten their deliverance.

Hear, O Lord, the prayers that we intend to offer Thee each day for the repose of the souls of the faithful departed, and grant to them rest, light, and peace. Hear also the prayers that these holy souls offer for us, so that we may obtain through their intercession the graces that we ask for. *Audi nunc, Domine, orationem mortuorum Israel.*

Month of the Holy Souls

FIRST DAY

ORIGIN OF THE DEVOTION TO THE MONTH OF THE FAITHFUL DEPARTED

I. The motives for sanctifying the month.
II. The means for sanctifying it well.

First Point.—If we wish to trace the origin of the devotion of the Month of the Faithful Departed, we shall find that it dates from the time of the Old Testament and of the people of Israel. They alone were guided by the Spirit of God, and not only did they not cease to proclaim in the Inspired Books, that *"it was a holy and wholesome thought to pray for the dead"* (2 Mach. 12:46); but they likewise made rules for the length of time that these prayers were to continue. In each family it was enacted, that the mourning should not cease, until a whole month had been passed in tears and supplications. Thus, when the Patriarch Jacob died, his sons wept and offered up prayers during the space of *thirty days.*

In later times, the faithful, stimulated by these ancient and well-authorized practices, have consecrated an entire month to the relief of the holy souls in Purgatory, and as the Church celebrates on the second of November the *Commemoration of the Faithful Departed,* this
month has been chosen as the most appropriate for the observance of the *Month of the Souls in Purgatory*; a devotion which has received the sanction of Sovereign Pontiffs, who have enriched it with spiritual favors.

Hail, then, with pleasure, O Christian soul, the dawn of this beautiful month, which answers so fully to the aspirations of your piety and the needs of your heart. It will recall to your mind the most tender family remembrances, the most sacred of promises, the most touching farewells. It will excite your compassion for relatives and friends, who because they are in misery and suffering, ought to be still dearer to you.

Yes, the dignity of these unfortunate souls, the intensity of their sufferings, their utter inability to help themselves, the glory of God, your own personal interest, all these press you to visit them, and come each day of this blessed month to their aid. Oh! is it not indeed the month of tears and lamentations, the month of charity and gratitude, the month of the living and of the dead, the month which may be truly named the *Month of Redemption.*

A saint, in a moment of enthusiasm, exclaimed, when commencing the devotions of the Month of November: "Let us empty Purgatory!"

Less ambitious, but not less zealous, say, O Christian soul, to yourself: I am determined to relieve many souls in Purgatory during this month; consecrated to them. I will do it, I ought to do it, and I can do it!

Second Point.—In order to celebrate well this Month of the Faithful Departed, make today the following resolutions and observe them faithfully. Each morning offer to God for the Souls in Purgatory, all the merits of your different works, of your sufferings and of your good deeds. Say, on first waking, O God, I offer everything to Thee, for thy greater glory and the relief of my deceased relatives, Arrange a fixed hour for reading attentively the daily chapter of the Month of the Souls in Purgatory; it will enlighten your mind and touch your heart, and be careful never to omit it. Go sometimes, if you have an opportunity, to the cemetery and offer a prayer for the repose of those you loved, who lie buried there. Set apart one day in each week to pray more especially for the souls in Purgatory. Take for instance *Wednesday,* and on that day hear Mass for this intention, In the course of the month give an alms to the poor, and offer several fervent Communions for the holy souls.

Do this, O Christian soul, and at the end of the month you will have sent to join the Church Triumphant in Heaven, a great number of souls who now weep and mourn in the flames of (the Church Suffering in) Purgatory. What a subject of consolation and of hope will not this be to you! "Arise," says St. Bernard, "hasten to the relief of the souls of the
dead, by your supplications; invoke the divine clemency for them; by your tears implore mercy for them; by your prayers intercede for them; by the Sacrifice of the Mass make satisfaction for them; ransom them with your alms and good works, and open to them the gates of heaven."

EXAMPLE

The following account of a wonderful cure obtained through the intercession of the Souls in Purgatory during the Month of November is perfectly authentic: –

"During several years," said the narrator of the fact, "I suffered from a very painful illness, which reduced my body to a skeleton, and my life was little else than a martyrdom, which could only end in the grave. I had consulted eminent medical men, but their remedies, with rare exceptions, gave no relief. I became still weaker, and finding I had nothing to hope for from science, I laid aside all remedies and determined to have recourse to the souls in Purgatory, who understand so well the mystery of suffering.

The month of November, which is especially consecrated to them, was about to begin, and I resolved to observe it with all possible fervor and end with a good communion. My relatives and many pious friends joined their prayers to mine. Every day towards evening we met at the foot of a statue of St. Joseph, and we asked with great confidence for two things–the deliverance of the poor souls in Purgatory and my cure. Towards the end of the first week I felt myself really better, and the last day of this blessed month I was able to go to church, and full of gratitude receive Holy Communion.

My cure was complete; no trace was left of the painful illness from which I had suffered so long and which the physicians had pronounced as incurable. Unbounded thanks be rendered to the Holy Souls of Purgatory whose protection in my regard was so manifest and so visible.

What favors may we not also obtain for our dear departed and ourselves, if we devoutly celebrate this month. Let us, then, have courage and confidence.

PRAYER

Good and merciful God, deign to grant the fervent prayers that we offer Thee during this month of blessings. We resolve to consecrate every day and every hour of it to the relief and deliverance of the captive souls who cry to Thee and to us from the depths of their dark dungeon. Lord, call Thy children and our brethren to eternal repose, and may perpetual light shine upon them. May they rest in peace!—*Requiescant in pace.*

SECOND DAY

PURGATORY

I. What is Purgatory?
II. For what reason is there a Purgatory?

First Point.—Faith teaches us that Purgatory, as the meaning of the word indicates, is a place of suffering and expiation, where Divine Justice completes the purification of the souls of the faithful, who are not sufficiently guilty to be condemned eternally to the flames of hell, nor pure enough to be admitted to heaven. Purgatory, then, is not heaven, where nothing defiled can enter in; nor hell from which there is no deliverance; it is an intermediate place between the abode of everlasting joys and the abode of everlasting sorrows. It partakes of the nature of hell on account of the intensity of its sufferings, and it partakes of the nature of heaven on account of the holiness of the sufferers. It is a prison, but not an eternal one; it is a fire that consumes yet purifies; it is an abode of tears, but the tears are not the *eternal* tears spoken of in Scripture. When the work of purgation is ended, when God shall have no

7

further claims against these debtors freed by suffering, He will call them to Himself to make them partakers of His own happiness. Purgatory is, then, a temporary place of suffering, and after the Day of Judgment it will no longer exist. Some of the Doctors of the Church think that it is placed in the center of the earth, very near to hell. They call it a lower place, a deep pit, a land of misery and darkness.

Such is Purgatory, and it is there that the greater portion of souls who have finished their pilgrimage on earth suffer and weep; for immediate entrance into heaven is, according to the opinion of learned theologians, a privilege granted but to few. There, in all probability, are the relatives, the benefactors, the friends whose loss we still mourn. It is there, O Christian soul, that you will very likely one day be, and that perhaps before long. Who is there that can flatter himself that he will die so pure as to have nothing to expiate? Oh, how necessary is it to understand the state of the poor souls in order to compassionate their sufferings, and thus merit to obtain relief for ourselves when our turn comes.

Second Point.— When a soul at the hour of death appears before the Sovereign Judge, Jesus, if it is pure from spot or stain, opens the gates of heaven and shows it the crown promised to those who conquer. If, on the contrary, it is found guilty of but a single mortal sin, that same moment is the decree of eternal reprobation pronounced. But what will become of the soul whose robe of innocence is tarnished with only some slight stain? Where will it go? What will become of those numberless souls who are not sufficiently pure to enter heaven, and who are not guilty enough to be condemned to hell? Will they never see the face of God? O let us bless God who, in his wisdom, has found the means of conciliating the claims of justice with those of mercy, by placing Purgatory as a middle place between heaven and hell.

It is there that souls are purified, as gold in the crucible, and it is there that the rust and stains of sin are effaced. Tertullian, in speaking of the sufferings
endured in Purgatory, calls them the torments of mercy—*Tormenta misericordiae.*

Consider, then, O Christian soul, that there is a reason for Purgatory. Yes; it is necessary, in order to complete the penance which has not been done in this world, to satisfy the Divine Justice, and to merit by expiation an immense weight of glory. It is an invention of the goodness of God, that might almost be called an eighth sacrament, *the sacrament of fire;* for those souls to whom the seven sacraments of the Church were not sufficient to confer on them perfect purity. All glory, then, to Divine Mercy which saves by Purgatory those we have loved, and which has placed in our hands the means for shortening their sufferings and opening for them the gates of heaven.

EXAMPLE

A zealous preacher, when terminating a discourse on Purgatory, expressed himself in these words: "A few days ago I received the news of the death of a venerable old man who in life had been a true Catholic, and the pattern of every Christian virtue. This old man was my father, and far from him as I am, the news has broken my heart, for I had not the happiness to see him once more and with my priestly hand close his eyes. In my grief I have but one consolation left, and that is, I have it in my power to succor his soul by offering up Mass for him, and I am able also to recommend him, as I do now recommend him, to your good prayers. When I approach the altar to offer the holy sacrifice for the repose of the soul of my dearly loved father, it seems to me that I have not lost him; it seems to me that he thanks me for this act of filial piety. He blesses me affectionately as he used to bless me when alive. It seems to me that my prayer shortens his sufferings, delivers him from Purgatory, and opens heaven to him—that heaven where he had so often told me to meet him. O what a holy and wholesome thought it is to pray for the dead. How truly is Purgatory an invention of God's mercy."

PRAYER.

I adore, O my God, thy eternal decrees, and I confess that Purgatory, in conciliating thy justice and mercy, is an invention of thy love. Grant, O Lord, that, by doing penance here on earth, I may escape the pains and privations of Purgatory, and that, through my prayers, I may obtain from thy paternal mercy that the suffering souls may speedily be united to Thee whom they love so ardently. O Jesus, be merciful to them; call thy children and thy brethren to eternal rest, and may perpetual light shine upon them. May they rest in peace.—*Requiescant in pace.*

THIRD DAY

THE EXISTENCE OF PURGATORY

I. The Word of God.
II. The teaching of the Church.

First Point.—The existence of Purgatory is not merely a pious belief that we are free to believe or disbelieve, it is a dogma of the Church, taught by faith, which we are bound to believe under pain of anathema. Yes; the Old Testament pronounces it to be "a holy and wholesome thought to pray for the dead, that they may be loosed from their sins" (2 Mach. 12:46), and so convinced were the Jews of this truth, that their ritual contained a special prayer for the deliverance of departed souls, which the head of each family was bound to recite before commencing meals.

Let us also hearken to the words of Christ: *"Be at agreement with thy adversary betimes, whilst thou art in the way with him, lest, perhaps, the adversary deliver thee to the judge, and the judge deliver thee to the officer, and thou be cast into prison."*

"Amen, I say to thee, thou shalt not go out from thence till thou repay the last farthing." According to St, Augustine this adversary is no other than God Himself, the irreconcilable enemy of sin. This inexorable judge is Jesus Christ, who is called in Scripture the *Judge of the living and the dead;* and the prison—so much to be feared—is Purgatory, which no soul can quit until it has fully satisfied Divine Justice.

Jesus Christ was not content to engrave on our hearts the remembrance of Purgatory. He gave us also the proof; for after his death, He descended into Limbo to console and deliver the souls of the Patriarchs.

I believe, O God, in Purgatory, the same as I believe in all the dogmas that Thou hast taught; because Thou canst not deceive nor be deceived. I adore the equity of thy judgments, even in the
severity of thy justice. *Credo.*

Second Point.—The teaching of the Church is no less explicit as regards this article of faith, and, in the Council of Trent expresses herself in these words:—*"If any one saith, that, after the grace of justification has been received, to every penitent sinner the guilt is remitted and the debt of eternal punishment is blotted out in such wise, that there remains not any debt of temporal punishment to be discharged, either in this world, or in the next in Purgatory, before the entrance to the kingdom of heaven can be opened to him, let him be anathema,"* (Sess. vi., Can. 30). The Greek and Latin Fathers, as well as ancient and modern nations, have all professed the same belief.

In accordance with this article of Faith, the Church—our tender and compassionate Mother—prays daily for the souls in Purgatory, and concludes all her offices with this cry of anguish and of hope—*Eternal rest give to them, O Lord.* Moreover, she obliges all priests to make a memento for them in the Mass, and recommends her children to offer of tell to God their prayers, alms, and satisfactory works for the deliverance of their departed brethren. Lastly, the Church has appointed the 2nd of November as a solemn anniversary, on which day she calls all Christian nations to come to the relief of the souls of the departed.

How consoling is it, O Christian soul, to think that, after our death, the Church will pray for us; that she will invite all the faithful to petition God for our deliverance, and that she will not cease to pray for us until we are received into the bosom of the Church Triumphant. O Holy Catholic Church, how truly art thou a mother to us, and how well thou knowest the weakness of thy children.

EXAMPLE

Judas Machabeus had been appointed by the Lord to defend Israel, the law, Jerusalem, and its temple, and, after gaining a great victory and putting to flight the enemies of God and his country, the first act of this brave and pious warrior was to kneel in thanksgiving to the God of Armies. Rising afterwards, he saw around him the bodies of his soldiers who had been slain in the victorious battle, and, penetrated with a holy respect for the mortal remains of these valiant men, Judas had them taken for burial to the sepulchers of their fathers. Then, being mindful of the souls of these martyrs to religion and their country, he collected alms and sent twelve thousand drachmas of silver to Jerusalem to obtain a sacrifice for the sins of those who had died, for he wisely and piously thought of the resurrection, knowing that a great reward was reserved for those who died for the cause of God and religion.

This is what occurred on a battlefield in Palestine, more than two thousand years ago and, in confirmation of this practice—under the old law of praying for the dead—the inspired Word of God tells us that, "*It is, therefore, a holy and wholesome thought to pray for the dead, that they may be loosed from sins"* (2 Mach, 12:46). It is clear, then, that Judas Machabeus believed in Purgatory, and that the Holy Spirit confirmed the belief. Alas! where, in these days, shall we find Generals capable of imitating so pious an example!

PRAYER.

As a true child of the Catholic Church, I firmly believe, O my God, in the existence of Purgatory. I believe it, because it has been revealed by the Spirit of Truth, and taught by the Saints and Fathers of the Church. Increase my faith, so that my charity may also increase towards the captive souls. O Jesus, be merciful to them! Grant them, O Lord, eternal rest and let perpetual light shine upon them. May they rest in peace.—*Requiescant in pace.*

FOURTH DAY

THE EXISTENCE OF PURGATORY

I. The testimony of our reason.
II. The testimony of our heart.

First Point.—Reason, in accordance with faith, proclaims also the existence of Purgatory, and speaks to us not less dearly than Scripture and the Church. It tells us that God being holiness itself, nothing defiled can enter into his kingdom; between the greatest good and the smallest evil there is an insurmountable barrier, and that a soul if stained by any spot however slight, is unworthy to be united to Him, until it undergoes purification. If this were not so, sin would for the first time, be introduced into Heaven. "O *Lord,*" exclaims the Royal Prophet, *"who shall dwell in Thy tabernacle, or who shall rest in thy holy hill? He that walketh without blemish and worketh justice"*(Ps. 14:1, 2).

Reason tells us also that God being infinitely just, He exacts reparation; that He can no more leave sin unpunished than He can leave unrewarded the smallest act of virtue. It follows then, that he who has not satisfied for his sins in this world, will infallibly have to satisfy for them in the next. The satisfactions that we shall have omitted rendering to the justice of God during this life, the justice of God will render to itself after our death, and where else can this be done but in Purgatory.

Christian soul, let us prove our faith in the dogma of Purgatory, by practicing a tender charity for the holy souls who are undergoing its torments, and by the avoidance of those slight faults which will lead us to it. *"He that is just, let him be justified still: and he that is holy let him be sanctified still."* (Apoc. 22:11.)

Second Point.—Every dogma of Catholicity, said Count De Maistre, has its roots in the depths of the human heart, and, for this reason, we find ourselves naturally inclined to believe certain revealed truths. Of these, Purgatory is one. Even those impious men who have abjured every belief and every feeling of religion, own truthfully that in moments of bereavement they cannot refrain from offering, in secret, prayers for those to whom they had been tenderly united. In all nations and in every country are these feelings to be met with, proving that by the hand of God alone have they been imprinted on the human heart. And what greater consolation can there be than this belief, than these pious practices, which unite us in thought to the sufferings of the dead? Yes, it becomes a necessity for us to believe that beyond the grave there exists a place of expiation that is not hell, but the way to Heaven. It becomes a necessity for us to believe that our relatives and friends who are the prisoners of Divine Justice, are helped by our prayers and good works, that they see and hear us, and that one day, when our turn comes, we also shall experience the same relief. How much are Protestants to be pitied, for their religion speaks not to their hearts. "O holy Catholic Church," exclaimed a venerated prelate, " true religion of the heart, how I love to see thee dispelling the dark clouds of grief, brightening sorrow with a ray of sunshine, and casting flowers on our funeral path."

EXAMPLE

A young Scotch Presbyterian had an only brother to whom he was much attached, and who met his death very suddenly. He had joined a party bent on pleasure, and was struck with apoplexy in the midst of his companions, who had little expected such an occurrence. Ever after the sad event the young Scotchman gave way to melancholy. He thought incessantly of the sudden transition from worldly festivities to the dread tribunal of God's judgment, and he feared that his brother would not have been sufficiently free from stains of sin, to entitle him to enter at once into the Kingdom of Heaven, and the Protestant religion showed him no intermediate place between Heaven and the abyss of hell.

To divert his mind from the melancholy which oppressed him, he was ordered to travel. In one of his journeys in France, he met a priest to whom he told the subject of his grief.

"My good friend," said the priest, "you will never find either comfort or hope except in the Catholic religion, which is so admirably adapted to the needs of the human heart; that Church tells us that there exists between heaven and hell a third place, where souls finish their purification and where we can help them by our prayers. You, as a Protestant, do not believe in this, and are deprived of the consolations it affords; but become a Catholic and you will then be able to pray for your beloved brother; you will hold converse with him, and each day you will pray for his admittance into heaven. Then and then only will you be freed from the grief which oppresses you."

The young man followed the advice that had been given him. He made his abjuration and was received into the Church, and as a true Catholic was often seen kneeling in prayer by his brother's grave. How true it is, that the belief in Purgatory is a necessity for the human heart.

PRAYER

Yes, O God! my heart needs the assurance that death does not put an end to intercourse with those from whom it separates me, and that my prayers and tears can plead with Thee for them, and hasten their entrance into eternal happiness. Blessed be Thou for making an article of faith, what is to us so great a consolation. O Jesus, show mercy to the faithful departed in the dwelling-place of eternity. May they rest in peace!—*Requiescant in pace.*

FIFTH DAY

THE SUFFERING OF PURGATORY
THE PAIN OF FIRE

I. A real Fire.
II. A Fire of vengeance.

First Point.—The great Apostle St. Paul tells us that there are souls who will not be admitted into the realms of bliss, until they have been purified by fire, *quasi per ignem.* But it is not the fire of hell of which he speaks, which will never be extinguished; it can, therefore, be no other than the fire of Purgatory; and this is the unanimous belief of all the great Doctors of the Church. If we consult Saint Ambrose, Saint Augustine, and Saint Thomas, as to what are the sufferings of the souls in Purgatory, they will answer with one voice, that it is the pain of fire. And were it permitted to us to bend over the brink of that abyss, to listen to the plaints of those we love, we should hear suffering voices crying to us from the depths of Purgatory, in the words of the rich man who was condemned to hell: "*I am tormented in this flame*" (Luke, 16:24) *Crucior in hâc flammâ.*

Fire, then, O Christian soul, is the torment. To be entirely immersed in fire, in an active, penetrating fire, which reaches to the inmost being. Oh what an excruciating torment! Material fire acts only on the body and yet how terrible are its effects! Who is there who would hold a burning coal in his hand for the space of a minute? But the fire of Purgatory acts on the soul; it reaches to the intellect, to the memory, to the senses; it pervades and penetrates every faculty: *anima tota punitur.* Figure to yourself this torment which we can scarcely imagine, though we have so often merited it by our daily faults, and let us in the words of Scripture ask ourselves this question: "*which of you can dwell with devouring fire?*" (Isai. 33:14.) O God, preserve us from the fire of Purgatory, deliver the souls who suffer there! and with the heavenly dew of thy love extinguish the flames which are devouring them.

Second Point.—In order to understand the intensity of the fire of Purgatory, we must remember that it was enkindled and is maintained by the breath of God's justice; that it does not act as an element but as the instrument of Divine power; and it tortures its victims the more, as it acquires a strength from the anger of

God, which it could not of itself possess, in order that it may punish souls without causing death and may purify without destroying. The fire of this world is a gift of Providence, whereas that of Purgatory is a creation of God's justice, of his anger, of his vengeance. St. Thomas says: "that the most burning furnaces and sharpest fires to which the martyrs were condemned, are nothing in comparison to the devouring flames that are suffered in Purgatory." This fire, says a holy Father, is like unto that of hell, except in its duration. Oh, how terrible is the suffering, and how great a martyrdom do not these poor victims endure!

Remember, O Christian soul, that the sufferings of this life—whatever they may be—are nothing in comparison to those of Purgatory. Who is there so hardhearted as not to hearken to the pitiable cries of these unfortunate beings who implore our help from the depths of the
prison where they burn day and night? Oh! were you in their place, and others had as little charity as you have for the poor souls, by what name would you call such cruelty? Reflect seriously and resolve to act differently in future.

EXAMPLE

A few years ago, in a town in France, a fire broke out in the basement floor of a house. It was during the night, and several people were sleeping in the upper rooms, but so soundly that they did not wake till the fire gained the floor beneath where they slept. Escape was then impossible; the bystanders were powerless to help and could only watch the frantic efforts of the victims and hear the despairing cries of "Save, oh, save us!" Meanwhile the flames reached the roof, which fell in, burying the unfortunate inmates.

Heartrending as was the scene, there is yet another still more sad and painful, which we little heed. The souls of our friends and relatives are being devoured by fire, and by what fire?—by a fire enkindled by the wrath of God. You can save them by your tears and the merits of Jesus Christ. Oh, have pity on them; save them, Jesus, have mercy on them!

PRAYER

O God, how greatly do I dread thy justice, when I recall to my remembrance the sensual life I have led; my many sins, and the little I have done for Thee! Have mercy on me, O God, and have mercy also on the souls of my relatives who have gone before me into eternity and who are now in the dominion of thy justice. O Jesus, be merciful to them; deliver thy children and our brethren from the avenging flames, and admit them to the realms of bliss. May they rest in peace.—*Requiescant in pace.*

SIXTH DAY

THE PAIN OF THE LOSS OF GOD

I. The privation of God.
II. The privation of heaven.

First Point.—Fire, terrible as it is, is not the principal suffering of Purgatory. There is another still greater, which theologians call the pain of loss. Here, on earth, we do not understand how great is the torture of the privation of God, because we see Him not; we do not love Him with our whole hearts, and we seldom think of Him. But the souls in Purgatory have seen God at the hour of death. As St. Ambrose expresses it, *a great spectacle* was offered to their sight. God manifested Himself to them with all his infinite perfections, imprinted his image clearly on their minds, and surrounded them with the splendors of His Majesty, so that the thought of Him is ever present to their hearts, and they love Him with a pure and undivided love. This insatiable love, this privation, this hunger and thirst of God overwhelms and tortures them; they are, as it were, ever dying, without being able to die; expiring, and yet unable to expire. With good reason the Church names the state of these souls as *death.* "Lord," does she exclaim, "deliver them from death." *Libera eas a morte!*

In order to understand, O Christian soul, the greatness of this torture, represent to yourself a man who is dying of suffocation. See his struggles and the efforts he makes in order to breathe; mark how his chest heaves and swells; it is a terrible struggle between life and death. But what is a little air in comparison to God, who is the air and breath of souls? What a living hunger, what a painful agony! O Lord, Lord, deliver them from eternal death. Let them see thy adorable face. *Libera eas a morte.* O Father, who art in heaven, take unto Thee thy exiled children!

Second Point.—Truly is the soul in Purgatory exiled—exiled not only from its earthly country, but from heaven, its true country. The soul had a glimpse from afar of the splendors of this heavenly country, when, on quitting this vale of tears, it appeared before Jesus Christ, who forms the joy and happiness of the elect. And it had a foreshadowing of what it was, when it recalled the invitation addressed to the souls of the just: *"Come, ye blessed of my Father, p08sess you the kingdom prepared for you from the foundation of the world."* (Matt. 25:34.) Momentarily had it seen the magnificence of heaven; but, unable to reach this s0 much wished-for country, the poor soul must wait days—years perhaps, centuries—before it can wing its flight to heaven, before it can be immersed in the torrent of happiness.

Hearken to the touching plaints of the unfortunate soul: "When shall I—poor exile that I am—see my true country and my family who are in heaven? Jerusalem, Jerusalem! Orphan that I am, when shall I join my parents, my brothers, my sisters, who are in the possession of glory, and whose hands are stretched out to me! When shall I be united to Jesus, my heavenly Spouse! O eternal gates, open, open!" But, alas, a mysterious voice replies: "Not yet awhile, but later!"

Christian soul, you have it in your power to open these gates, for, do you not know that prayer and alms are the golden keys which open heaven? Oh! pray, and pray often; give much, and the exiled souls of Purgatory will ascend to their happy country, where they chant eternally the mercies of the Lord.

EXAMPLE

When the children of Israel, led captive, far away from their own country, could only see the banks of the Euphrates, they seated themselves mournfully on the unknown soil and wept over the remembrance of their lost Jerusalem. *Illic sedimus et flevimus dum recordaremur Sion.* No longer in their midst were heard joyous words and canticles; their harps, hung on the willows that grew on the banks of the river, were silent.

"Children of Israel, why weep ye?" asked the Babylonians.

"We weep," was the answer, "because we think of Sion our country; we remember it, and we mourn for it!"

"But, exiled sons of Sion, why sing you not to soften your grief and distract your melancholy thoughts! . . . Sing! sing some of the canticles of your country—sing your national hymn."

"Sing, alas! Can the exile sing his country's hymns in a stranger's land? Far from home and country he regrets, he mourns, he weeps, he awaits in tears the consolation of returning. O Jerusalem! Jerusalem! may my tongue cleave to my palate if one day I forget thee!"

And so, without doubt, does it come to pass when the souls of our brethren, retained by

Divine Justice, far from that country to which love calls them, reach the brink of the abyss

where expiation condemns them to a painful exile, they halt on those shores, a thousand times

more desolate than the shores of the earth: and there, filled with the thoughts of the heavenly country, they also weep that they are kept from it; but with tears, with lamentations that differ as much from our tears and sighs as heaven differs from earth, as time differs from eternity!

PRAYER

O my God, God so holy and so just, but so rich in mercy, let the love of these holy souls move Thee to compassion. Refuse no longer to grant their desires; repulse them not; open to them thy heart, and let them lose themselves in Thee. O Jesus, be merciful to them. Call, O Jesus, thy children and our brethren to eternal bliss, and let perpetual light shine upon them. May they rest in peace.—*Requiescant in pace.*

SEVENTH DAY

THE PAIN OF REMORSE

I. The evil that had to be avoided.
II. The good that had to be done.

First Point.—The torments we have already spoken of are not, alas! the only ones with which the souls detained in the place of expiation are tortured. They suffer sadness, desolation, bitter regrets, and the cutting reproaches of a guilty conscience, which are a thousand times more difficult to bear than the pains of the material fire which burns without consuming.

In hell, as Scripture tells us, *"their worm dieth not."* Not so in Purgatory, there it will one day die, but so long as it lives, its bite is cruel, and it tears its unfortunate victim, whose executioner it has become. Oh! how terrible is the struggle of a soul that is weighed down with remorse! From the depths of its dungeon the captive soul casts a mournful look on its former life, and by the light of the flames which surround it, it sees distinctly all the evil it has committed and which, with the grace of God, it could so easily have avoided. It sees clearly thousands of faults which in life had passed unheeded, or had not been considered serious. Compelled to acknowledge itself guilty, the poor soul, who had it in its power to be righteous, is overwhelmed with grief, and in the excess of its sorrow, cries out: O God, Thou art just and Thy judgments are just; I alone am the cause of my sufferings. Could I but recommence my life, how well would I serve Thee, O Lord, and with what care would I avoid Purgatory! But these regrets are useless, alas, it is too late; too late!

Christian soul, let this be a lesson to us to avoid sin, and do penance here on earth, so as to escape these pains, this never-dying worm of Purgatory. Let us say with St. Augustine: "Here cut, here burn, spare me not here, O Lord, provided Thou sparest me eternally."

Second Point.—What increases greatly the sufferings of the exiled soul, is the sight of all the good it might have done, and that it has so often omitted; the recollection of all the favors it has received from God's bounty, but which it did not always make a good use of. In a word what could the Lord do more to make it bring forth the fruits of salvation? He had given it the gift of the true faith, He had nourished it with the Sacraments, fortified it by his grace, and encouraged it by good examples. With so many helps it ought to have advanced with a giant's step in the path of sanctity, and have reached, as so many others had done, the highest perfection. But, notwithstanding all these aids, the unhappy soul, not only advanced slowly, but often halted. Oh! had it been but a little generous, and inflicted on itself a small penance, or some slight mortification; If even it had accepted with resignation the inevitable pains of life, it would have had its Purgatory upon earth, and at death would have enjoyed the beatific vision for eternity. But now it has to endure, through its own fault and without merit, incomparably greater sufferings. Instead of a crown of glory, that It might have had in heaven, it is tortured in Purgatory by a crown of flames. Oh, what an afflicting thought! and what a sharp sting of remorse will not this be! .

Christian soul, enter into yourself and see if you also do not feel remorse of conscience and very bitter regrets? The regret of having committed much evil and done but little good. The regret for having prayed so little for the relief of the souls of your deceased relatives. Delay not to make a firm resolution, with the assistance of God and the Blessed Virgin, to do better for the time to come.

EXAMPLE

Gerson, Chancellor of the University of Paris, who was as renowned for virtue as he was for eloquence, relates in one of his writings, that a mother who had been long forgotten by her son, was permitted by God to appear to him, to tell her sufferings and solicit his prayers.

"My son," exclaimed she, "my dear son, think a little of your poor mother, who suffers so much. Reflect on the frightful torments which Divine Justice makes me endure in expiation for the sins of my mortal life. But the greatest of all these torments is *remorse,* the deep regret I feel for having loved God so little, who had granted me so many graces; for having offended so great, so holy a God, so enlightened a Judge, such a tender Father, such a generous benefactor. Oh, it is this thought which overwhelms and kills me at every moment; this gnawing worm is like to a sharp dagger which stabs without causing death, which tortures day and night, and draws from me tears of blood. At the same time I am forced to cry out in striking my breast: 'My God, Thou art just; if I suffer cruelly it is through my own fault, through my very great fault.' O my son, if you still love me, take pity on me, draw out this dagger, deliver me from the worm that gnaws me, and open heaven to me. One other thing I ask of you, my loved son, serve God better than your mother did, and when death comes, die with tears of repentance and a contrite heart."

The youth was faithful to his mother's warnings; he prayed much for her, and he himself died the death of the just.

PRAYER

Grant me, O God, the grace. to become as holy and as perfect as Thou dost wish me to be. The souls in Purgatory are severely punished by the upbraidings of regret for having been negligent. Soften their remorse, O Lord, by forgiving their faults; for the sword that stabs them is too sharp. O Jesus, have mercy on them, call Thy children and our brethren to the possession of glory. May they rest in *peace.—Requiescant* in p*ace.*

EIGHTH DAY

DURATION OF THE PAINS OF PURGATORY

I. What is the duration?
II. What are the causes?

First Point.—Though the Church has not defined anything as to the duration of the pains of Purgatory, yet the fact of allowing anniversaries to be kept and Masses to be said in perpetuity, for the repose of the souls of the dead, shows what is her belief regarding it. She thinks, then, that expiation must be long, and may even be prolonged through centuries. The same is the opinion of the Fathers of the Church. St. Augustine asked for prayers for his mother, St. Monica, after she had been dead more than twenty years, and St. Ambrose promised publicly to pray all his life for the soul of the Emperor Theodosius the Great. Cardinal Bellarmine says that, according to trustworthy revelations, the pains of Purgatory, in regard to certain souls, might last till the Day of Judgment, if the Church did not come to their assistance. From this it will appear that there are poor souls who have been suffering during long years. Who can tell us the length of time, and the amount of suffering that is requisite to expiate one venial sin, or to cleanse the rust left by mortal sin on the soul, and restore it to the brilliant beauty of the angels? Oh, unfathomable mystery of the judgments of God!

It is well known that length of time adds much to the severity of suffering. To suffer terribly and for a long time! to wait and wait for the end! to have to wait an indefinite time! Oh, what a painful martyrdom must not this be to these poor souls! Added to this, the intensity of the sufferings they endure, makes moments appear like months, and months like ages. Oh, how incomprehensible are these tortures of lengthened hours and ages! Shorten, O Lord, these agonies, put an end to the intensity and duration of the sufferings of our friends and relatives, especially of those who would otherwise have to remain the longest in this place of expiation.

Second Point.—We must not be surprised at the terrible duration of the torments of Purgatory. A very holy nun of the Order of the Visitation, Sister Mary Denis, who was well known to have been favored with extraordinary graces for the relief of departed souls, said that there were many causes why the long duration of suffering in Purgatory was inevitable. First the inconceivable purity which is required of a soul before it can possess God; secondly, the innumerable multitude of venial sins; thirdly, the little penance that is done for mortal sins that have been confessed; fourthly, the absolute incapability of the souls of the deceased to do anything for their own relief; and fifthly, the forgetfulness that exists for the dead, and the culpable negligence in obtaining relief for them. All this is unfortunately but too true.

In future we must be careful to avoid a very common fault, and that is to regard those we love, who die, as being already saints. So consoling is it to believe them in a place of peace and happiness, that we try to convince ourselves they are already there, and then we cease to weep and pray for them. The saints acted very differently. All their lives they prayed for those that death had taken from them, and even when dying they with tears entreated prayers for them. Let us do in like manner. We who cannot hold a finger in the fire for the space of a minute without crying out with pain, how is it that we can allow the souls of those we loved so much to remain, through our negligence, for the space of many years, in the devouring flames of Purgatory. No, loved souls, we will not be so cruel, we at least, will never forget you!

EXAMPLE

The simple narration of the following historical event, speaks more eloquently than the longest discourse:

A man who, for five years, had been confined in a well-known prison, worn out by suffering, conceived at length a project for his deliverance. At that time a woman had great power, and her influence was so great, that she was able to break the prisoner's chains and bring his sufferings to an end. History relates that the petition he addressed to her was couched in these words: "Madame, the 25th of this month, 1760, I shall have been suffering a hundred thousand hours, and there yet remains two hundred thousand hours more suffering before my sentence ends. Oh! Madame, let your heart be moved by such a long and painful martyrdom."

I know not if this woman was hard-hearted enough to resist such an eloquent appeal, but it would seem impossible to express more in so few words. I have been suffering a hundred thousand hours, and there remains yet two hundred thousand more to suffer. There are two hundred thousand more! . . . He had then counted the hours! Yes, as we should count one by one the strokes of a clock's pendulum during a long night, when pain and suffering prevented sleep!

And thus it is that the poor souls in Purgatory calculate the duration of their sufferings, but not by hours or by days do they count, it is by years, and these years appear to them as ages. O justice of God, how terrible art thou! O poor souls who have suffered so long, how I pity you!

PRAYER

Struck with terror at the thoughts of the severity of Thy judgments and the length and intensity of the sufferings which Thy justice inflicts on the poor souls in Purgatory, I kneel at Thy feet, great God, and full of compassion for the unfortunate prisoners, I implore Thee in the name of Jesus Christ, to cast on them a look of mercy and put an end to their sufferings. O Mary, comforter of the afflicted, be merciful to them, and deliver thy children from captivity. May they rest in peace near to thee in Heaven.—*Requiescant in pace.*

NINTH DAY

THE HELPLESSNESS OF THE SOULS IN PURGATORY

I. Their sufferings are unavailing.
II. Their prayers are unavailing.

First Point.—consider that all merit ceases at the hour of death, for the soul, unable any more to combat, has no longer free choice between good and evil. Purgatory is the night spoken of by Jesus Christ when none can labor. Those who suffer there are like the husbandman in the Gospel, who is prevented cultivating his field any longer. And in the same manner, the departed, who are so dear to us, can do nothing themselves to alleviate their sufferings. Their perfect resignation, their ardent love of God, the severity of their torments are of no avail, and will shorten the duration of them, even for a moment. In this life the least of the sufferings of Purgatory would have merited "a*n eternal weight of glory*";[1] but, in this terrible place of

---

[1] 2 Cor. 4:17.

expiation, sufferings are fruitless to the souls there imprisoned and fruitless for heaven; they are simply a payment of a debt that is due. What a terrible thought must it be for these dear souls, and how greatly must it add to their torments, to know and feel, that they will have to suffer cruelly, to suffer perhaps for ages, and to suffer without any profit to themselves. From us alone can they hope to receive either help or relief.

Yes, Christian soul, we alone can help the dead, we alone can be to them a liberating providence. The thought of heaven consoles them, but we relieve them; the thought of heaven encourages them, but we deliver them; the saints open their arms to receive them, but it is we who introduce them into the dwellings of bliss. This, then, is our power, and this is our duty, but do we often think of it?

Second Point.—Not only are the souls in Purgatory incapable of obtaining relief for themselves by their sufferings, but they cannot even help themselves by prayer. In vain, from the depths of the burning abyss, does their cry of anguish rise to God, in vain do they try to soften his justice, and say in the words of David, "My God, my God, why hast thou forsaken me? I shall cry by day and thou wilt not hear; and by night and it shall not be reputed as folly in me" (Ps. 21:1-3). Be mindful, O Lord, of Thy mercies, break the chains which retain me far from Thee; deliver me from the torments I endure. Alas, how long and painful is my exile! Be merciful to me, O Lord!

Deaf to their cries of distress, God replies: "The time of mercy is past, the reign of justice has begun. Your supplications are useless; you will not come forth from your prison until your debt has been paid by sufferings."

Powerless, then, as are the prayers of the departed, it is not so with our prayers, for they are all-powerful with the heart of Jesus, and, in proportion as they ascend to Heaven, mercy descends into Purgatory in torrents of grace, pardon, liberty, and glory. It was through prayer that Martha and Mary obtained the resurrection of Lazarus, and it is by prayer that we also shall obtain the deliverance of our departed relatives. Oh! Let us, then, pray with all our heart and pray unceasingly for them. Let us say often: "Good and merciful Jesus, grant them eternal rest. Mary, mother and comforter of the afflicted, hasten to help them. All ye saints of heaven, intercede for them."

EXAMPLE

The Redeemer, passing through Judea, saw one day a paralytic man seated mournfully beside the pool of Siloe. At certain times, "*an angel of the Lord descended into the pond and the water was moved, and he that went down first into the pond after the motion of the water was made whole*" (John, 5:4). The paralytic man spoken of in the Gospel had waited many years without being able to reach the water first, and the Savior, moved with compassion, drew near and asked why he did not descend with the others into the pond.

"Lord," replied he, "my limbs are paralyzed and I have no man to put me into the water. My much wished-for cure does not depend on myself, for I am paralyzed. I need a friend to assist me who will extend to me a helping hand." Poor paralyzed man, how greatly were you to be pitied!

Such, also, is the fate of the holy souls in Purgatory; they are powerless to move, incapable of helping themselves, incapable of casting themselves into the saving bath of the precious blood of Jesus, which has redeemed the world. Like the paralytic man in the Gospel, they wait for a friend to help them. Christian soul, be you that charitable friend. Oh, yes, be the delivering angel of the poor paralytics of Purgatory!

PRAYER

Permit me, O God, to recommend to Thee the poor souls, who, surrounded by darkness can in no way help themselves. Their prayers and tears cannot move Thee, but Thou hast permitted me to be their mediator, and to intervene between them and Thy justice. Oh! I implore Thee, remit their punishment and put an end to their painful exile. O Jesus, be merciful to them! Call Thy children and our brethren to Thyself, and may they rest in peace!—*Requiescant in pace.*

TENTH DAY

THE TWO ROADS WHICH LEAD TO PURGATORY

I. The road of mortal sin.
II, The road of venial sin.

First Point.—Mortal sin, by its nature, leads the soul beyond Purgatory; it predestinates it into the abyss of hell. But if the poor sinner approaches the Sacrament of Confession, and, by means of sacramental grace, his sins are forgiven, what will then happen to him? The mortal sin is forgiven, God's friendship is restored to him, and the eternal punishment of it is commuted into a temporal punishment, which must be expiated either in this world by penance, or in the next by the pains of Purgatory. And should it chance that a great sinner receives absolution, not of one mortal sin only, but of many—of ten, of a hundred, extending over many years—what a long, what a fearful Purgatory awaits him! What an enormous debt has he to pay to Divine Justice! It is true that the sacramental penance given in confession reduces the debt, but the penance enjoined is often very slight, and, unhappily, is performed with little fervor! It is also true that practicing mortifications, and gaining indulgences, can preserve and deliver us from Purgatory, but, alas! there are few Christians who fast or who mortify themselves. The most guilty are generally those who do the least penance; and how many are there who have not sufficient contrition for the gaining of indulgences. O God, how few there are who escape falling into this terrible abyss! So many sins, and so little reparation!

This consideration, O Christian soul, is sufficient to cause us to reflect seriously and shed tears of repentance, if unhappily our past life has been stained by mortal sin—if we have been treading this first path which leads to Purgatory. O Lord God, pierce Thou my flesh with Thy fear, for I am afraid of Thy judgments (Ps. 118:120). This thought should also induce us to pray much for those souls in Purgatory who are the most guilty.

Second Point.—There are souls who like St. Aloysius, have been preserved from grievous sin, but who are nevertheless debtors towards God, on account of the many venial sins they have committed. In truth, these sins are innumerable. Your life is, perhaps, one tissue of venial sins. How many useless thoughts and idle words, how many rash judgments, how many willful distractions in prayer, what vanity, what uncharitable conversations, and how much time wasted frivolously! Do you not offend God very frequently, even daily, under the pretext that they are only slight faults? Are you not often guilty of certain venial sins which might be called grievous, because they border upon mortal sin, and when do you do penance for them? If your life is so loaded with debts and so void of satisfactions, it is very evident that you are on the second path which leads directly to Purgatory. Alas! what long days, months, and years will you have to suffer in this terrible place of expiation: what a long and rigorous Purgatory will be yours!

Christian soul, reflect seriously, and say to yourself—I am determined to settle my accounts with God. I will profit by the time that his mercy grants me to satisfy his justice; and a little generosity and love will enable me to pay the debts I owe. This I can do, this I ought to do, and this I am determined to do. O ye charitable souls of Purgatory, come to my assistance; obtain for me the spirit of penance, and I will ask for you in return consolation and relief.

EXAMPLE

Nothing is more calculated to convince us of the malice of venial sin than the well-authenticated accounts of the apparitions of a great many souls, who have revealed how rigorously God has punished them for faults which they considered as only very slight.

Some have been condemned to Purgatory for having talked without necessity in church, as is related by St. Cesarius of a little girl, seven years old. Others, like the sister of St. Peter Damien, for having listened to a profane song. A noble Roman lady, named Catharine, died, of whom St. Monica entertained so high an opinion that, when she lived, she used often to recommend her son, St. Augustine, to her pious prayers. Nevertheless, the soul of the departed appeared to the holy Bishop, St. Martin, and said: "I am burning in the expiatory flames for having two or three times washed my face through vanity." St. Severin passed some years in Purgatory, on account of certain faults of negligence in saying the Divine Office. A child, nine years of age, was condemned for not having paid for or restored some trifling things he had taken. The father of a family remained five hundred years in the fire of Purgatory for neglecting the education of his children; and how many others are there who have been punished equally?

Oh, let us, then, understand, by the light of the dread fire of Purgatory, how great an evil it is to commit venial sin! Alas! instead of weeping over it, we commit it without scruple, by way of amusement. Happy those souls who, at the hour of death, can say, like St. Paul: "I bear the marks of the Lord Jesus in my body." (Gal. 6:17.)

PRAYER

How many faults, O my God, have I allowed myself to commit without feeling any remorse, treating them as mere trifles! If I did but reflect on the strict account I shall have one day to render to Thy Justice, how much more careful should I be. I beseech Thee to bear with my weakness, and animate me to more courage. Show mercy to my brethren of the Church Suffering. O Jesus, have pity on them, and open to them the gates of the Church Triumphant. May they rest in peace.—*Requiescant in pace.*

ELEVENTH DAY

THE HOLINESS OF THE SOULS IN PURGATORY

I. They love God.
II. They are loved by God.

First Point.—St. Catharine of Genoa says: "That every soul, by the fact of its being in Purgatory, is raised to a state of perfection and divine union, which might serve as a model to the greatest saint on earth." There is, then, in Purgatory an immense multitude of souls who have triumphed over their passions, who have conquered the world and the devil, who have practiced the most heroic virtue, and who left this world full of merits. These would shine like stars in the firmament of heaven if their robe had not been sullied by some speck of earthly dust. Yes, indeed, these souls are beautiful, holy, incapable of sinning, and dead to every imperfection. The least amongst them is worth more than all this universe. They love God above all things, entirely, and by necessity. This very love makes them love their sufferings and the justice which retains them in this place of expiation. In vain would the gates of heaven open for them; they would prefer to remain surrounded by flames rather than enter into glory with the smallest imperfection, and they cannot sufficiently thank their God for having prepared a place of expiation, in which they are permitted to acquire the radiant beauty suited to his spouses. With more truth than Job, in the midst of his affliction, can they repeat unceasingly: "Blessed be the name of the Lord." (Job, 1:21.)

Let us then show great compassion to these holy souls whilst they stand in need of our assistance. Before long things will change; these holy souls will become our protectors in heaven, our mediators with God, and they will return us gratefully, a hundred fold, all that we do for them in their day of affliction.

Second Point.—"If God," says a pious author, "loves us poor sinners, who are so full of imperfections and so devoid of virtue and merit, how infinitely dearer to Him must be the holy souls in Purgatory, who belong to Him forever, and in whom he sees the resplendent beauty of his elect." They are his spouses, his dear children, the heirs of his glory called to bless Him eternally in heaven. They may all be likened to precious stones destined for the edifice of the heavenly Jerusalem, on which the chisel of the sculptor is about to impart its finishing touch before they are ready for the place that was destined for them from all eternity. Yes! God loves them tenderly and contemplates them with love, desiring to unite Himself to them. His paternal heart feels for them in their sad exile, but his justice, which as well as his goodness has its rights, keeps them imprisoned until all their debts are paid. But, if a friend, a mediator, interposing between the chastisement and the fault, comes to cancel the debt and reconcile the erring child, what joy will not this be to the heart of their good and tender Father?

How many reasons do there, then, exist for us to love these blessed souls and to exercise great mercy towards them, they who are so worthy of all our sympathy! If we give an alms to a poor person we know not if he deserve it, or if it will make him more criminal and ungrateful. But it is otherwise with the souls in Purgatory. The ground on which our seed falls is not barren, each grain that we sow is a fruit for heaven and a blessing to ourselves. This thought should not fail to encourage us.

EXAMPLE

One day, when St. Gertrude was in a rapture, she beheld the soul of a nun whose life had been passed in the exercise of the greatest virtues. She appeared standing in the presence of God, clothed with the emblems of divine charity, but not daring to raise her eyes to the adorable face of the Savior. She stood like a criminal, her eyes cast down and showing by her bearing that she wished to retire and go far from her heavenly Master. St. Gertrude, astonished and wishing to know the reason of what appeared to her as so unaccountable, said: "God of all goodness, why do you not let this soul approach you?"

At these words our Lord opened his arms as if wishing to draw the soul to Him, but instead of advancing it respectfully retired. The saint, still more surprised, asked the soul of the nun why she withdrew from the embraces of so loving a Spouse, and she replied: "Because I am not yet purified from the stains which my sins have left on me, and if God, even, granted me, in the state in which I am, the power to enter heaven, I would not consent; for resplendent as I may appear to you I am not yet worthy to be the spouse of my Savior."

Thus it is, that the holy souls suffer willingly and with perfect resignation. They are so transformed in God that they would not, were it in their power, be released in the smallest degree from their torments; and they accept them with an ever-increasing joy, in proportion as they near the termination of their expiation. Oh! how worthy are they of our love, our sympathy, and our charity.

PRAYER

O God, who dost forgive sinners, and who willest the salvation of all men, cast a look of mercy on the souls in Purgatory. They are thy spouses, the children of thy predilection, they have loved Thee tenderly and have served Thee courageously. Show unto them thy face, O Jesus, be merciful to them. Call, O Lord, thy children and our brethren to eternal happiness and let perpetual light shine upon them. May they rest in peace.—*Requiescant in pace.*

TWELFTH DAY

THE STATE OF THE SOULS IN PURGATORY WITH REGARD TO OURSELVES

I. They are united to us by the bonds of charity.
II. They are united to us by the bonds of relationship.

First Point.—Remember that we are united to the holy souls by the links of a spiritual and divine chain. Like ourselves they have been created to the image of God, redeemed by the blood of Jesus Christ, regenerated by the waters of baptism, and are children of the same mother, the Church. Like ourselves, and perhaps even together with us, they have taken their places at the Eucharistic table and received the sacred pledge of eternal life. They carried with them to the next world the same hopes that are now sweetening the bitterness of our pilgrimage. Members of the same body, heirs of the same kingdom, they will one day be our companions in eternity. But between them and ourselves there is this difference; they are in misery, prisoners, martyrs, powerless to help themselves, and it is from us they expect help and consolation. We have become their debtors.

Are not these indisputable claims to our compassion and love? Oh, if children of the same family love each other tenderly; the sorrows of the one become the sorrows of all; and ought it not to be the same with the children of the Catholic Church? Where will our charity be, if we do not love these poor souls overwhelmed with afflictions? Would it be possible for us, as men, and above all as Christians, to be insensible to their pains? Let us love them as ourselves, let us love them as Jesus Christ has loved us, then shall we relieve and deliver them. "*My little children,*" writes St. John the Evangelist, shortly before his death, "*let us not love in word, nor in tongue, but in deed and in truth*" (1 John, 3:18).

Second Point.—There are many souls in Purgatory who are united to us by the ties of relationship, and, amongst the plaintive voices bewailing their sufferings, do we not distinguish accents which speak eloquently to our hearts? Yes, they are the voices of our relatives, and, perhaps, that of a brother, or sister who loved you tenderly and who with you formed the happiness of the domestic circle; or the voice of the loved child, the hope of the family, that you tried to snatch from death, and who, in its agony, held out to you its cold and feeble hand. Or, again, it is the voice of a husband or wife that love had united at the foot of the altar, and that death, alas! had separated; or the voice of a father, of a mother whose blood flows in your veins and whose death caused you such bitter tears! And this cry of kindred, these voices of members of your own family, what do they say to you? Oh listen: "Come, O my brother, my sister, my child, my spouse, my father, come to my assistance: *miseremini mei.* I have called you long, I have but you to trust to, and you come not. Oh! come then with your heart's affection, come with prayer, with your good works; come and deliver me from this burning abyss, come and give me heaven, God, and eternity!"

Christian soul, can you resist this cry of anguish? How can you not respond to this earnest appeal? Who knows but that we ourselves may have heaped these burning coals on the heads of those who loved us so much, and perhaps too much? What more pressing motives can we have to come to their assistance!

EXAMPLE

In the year 1874 a celebrated Jewish musician was converted by hearing a sermon on the Holy Eucharist, and, after receiving baptism, he resolved to forsake the world and enter a very strict Religious Order. Every day he passed several hours in adoration before the Blessed Sacrament, and in his prayers he prayed fervently for the conversion of his mother, towards whom he felt the most tender affection. The much desired conversion was however not obtained, and his mother died, adhering obstinately to her Jewish errors. Overwhelmed with anguish, the good son prostrated himself before the Tabernacle, and giving vent to his grief, exclaimed: "I owe all to Thee, O Lord, it is true; but, at the same time, is there anything that I have refused to Thee?—my youth, my worldly hopes, my success in life, my family joys, the rest I had earned, all these I sacrificed the moment I heard Thy voice, and I would even have given my blood, hadst Thou required it. And Thou, O Lord, Thou the eternal goodness, who hast promised to reward a hundredfold, Thou hast refused me the soul of my mother!! O God, I shall sink under this martyrdom, and murmurs rise unbidden to my lips."

Suddenly a mysterious voice was heard: "Man of little faith, thy mother is saved!"

"My mother saved! O God, it is not possible!"

"Yes, she is saved; know that thy prayer prevailed with Me; I received all those thou didst address to Me for thy mother, and in her last hour I was mindful of them. At the moment of her death I presented Myself to her, she saw Me and exclaimed: 'My Lord and my God!' Have courage, thy mother has escaped damnation, and thy fervent prayers will soon deliver her soul from the prison of Purgatory."

The Rev. Father Herman, for it was he, learnt soon after from a second apparition, that his mother was in heaven. Oh! let us pray much for our deceased relatives.

PRAYER

Show mercy, O Lord, to the souls of those to whom Thou hast united me by ties of affection, and whom Thou hast made it a duty for me to love. Yes, be merciful to the souls of my relatives, benefactors, and friends; may the prayers and tears I offer for them prevail with Thee. O Jesus; O Mary, be merciful to them, call thy children and our brethren to the place of rest, light, and peace. *Requiescant in pace.*

THIRTEENTH DAY

THE ABANDONED SOULS

I. Abandoned by their friends.
II. Abandoned by their relatives.

First Point.—Consider that in the depths of Purgatory there are souls who are entirely abandoned, in whom no one takes any interest, and who suffer without any consolations. The Church, it is true, never forgets any of its children, and the souls of whom we speak, share with all the others in the prayers that this tender mother addresses each day to God in favor of the departed; but besides these prayers which are offered for all, no other help comes to them from earth. In the first place they are abandoned by their friends who had promised, nay sworn an undying affection towards them. But as this affection was purely a human one, and mingled with much of self, it died away with the last sound of the funeral bell. What an addition to the sufferings of these poor prisoners is caused by their being so unexpectedly forsaken. Listen to the well-merited reproaches they address to those who so soon have forgotten the duties of friendship. *"Have pity on me, at least you my friends"* (Job, 19:21). *Saltem vos amici mei.* We gave you so many proofs of our affection and attachment on earth, and you gave us so many assurances that you loved us tenderly! When we were dying you promised, in bidding us farewell, that you would never forget us! But, alas! you think of us no more, not a prayer, not an alms, not a tear. You have banished the remembrance of us from your heart, because we are out of sight. Oh, how little are human affections to be depended upon which, as Bossuet says, vanish with the years.

Christian soul, may not these reproaches be truthfully addressed to you? Do you ever think of the friends of your youth that death has taken away, and who are, perhaps, suffering now for having loved you too much? St. Francis of Sales says: "These dear departed, we forget them far too much, and nevertheless in life they loved us so." Well may we fear to be forgotten in our turn, for it is written that he who forgets shall be forgotten—*Si quis ignorat ignorabitur*!

Second Point.—Abandoned by their friends, these poor souls of whom we speak, are in like manner forsaken by their relatives, either because they have outlived them, or because they have cast aside every feeling of charity and gratitude. Yes; they are forsaken by their father, their mother, their brothers, their sisters, and their heirs. On every side they look, they see nothing but forgetfulness. Forgetfulness of their lives; not even a sound or a word to recall them; forgetfulness of their names, for no one ever pronounces them; forgetfulness of their tombs, for no one visits them nor prays beside them; forgetfulness of their deaths, for no one mourns them any more; forgetfulness of their sufferings beyond the grave, for no one tries to alleviate them. Forgetfulness everywhere and forever. Poor souls, who can tell how long your sufferings will last. Who knows how much more time you have to spend in this terrible Purgatory, where no help comes to you? How much must this cruel forgetfulness add to their sufferings? With good reason may they cry out in the words of the Psalmist: "*My friends and my neighbors have drawn near and stood against me. And they that were near me, stood afar off* (Ps. 37:11, 12). *I am forgotten as one dead from the heart. I am become as a vessel that is destroyed* (Ps. 30:13). Like Jesus in the Garden of Gethsemani, they can say: "*I looked for one that would comfort me, and I found none*" (Ps. 68:21).

Christian soul, pray often, give alms, and offer Communions for the most abandoned souls. Be to them a father, a mother, a brother, a sister, a friend. Can you have a more worthy object for your zeal and charity? Some day they will pray for you, if, as is not improbable, your relations and your heirs forget and forsake you.

EXAMPLE

A frightful crime was committed some years ago in a country village. A young man, whose heart was corrupted by passion, had the brutality, aided by an accomplice, to attempt the murder of his mother, and, hoping to drown her, they threw her into a pond of muddy water. The poor woman struggled and stretched out her hands to her murderers, but the accomplice pushed her back when she tried to reach the bank. The son, villain as he was, when he saw his mother's arms extended towards him, the arms that had carried him when an infant, could not resist the voice of nature, and holding out his hand he endeavored to drag her to the bank, and in this would have succeeded had not his bloodthirsty companion suddenly forced her back into the water, where she sank.

In the invisible lake of Purgatory there will be found friends and relatives whom we could deliver, and who, alas! would not perhaps be there were it not through our fault. Yes, it is perhaps owing to us that a father, a mother, and brother are suffering in that lake of fire, and whilst we, unmindful of them, are busy in the pursuit of pleasure, they are struggling in frightful torments. They weep, they implore, they stretch forth their hands to us, and shall we not deliver them?

Poor souls, you are our sisters in Jesus Christ, we will be to you a father, a mother, a brother, and a sister, we will be your friends, your saviors, and the day will come when you also will come to our assistance.

PRAYER

O Jesus, abandoned by all, even by thy disciples, in the garden of Gethsemani, have pity on all the holy souls in Purgatory, and in particular on those for whom no one offers any special prayer, who receive no comfort from the living, and whose anniversaries pass unheeded. Be their consoler and deliverer. O Jesus, call thy abandoned children to the bosom of their heavenly family. May they rest in peace. *Requiescant in pace.*

FOURTEENTH DAY

MEANS FOR ASSISTING THE SOULS IN PURGATORY

I. We can assist them.
II. We ought to assist them.

First Point.—We believe, as is defined by the Council of Trent, that the souls who are detained in Purgatory can be helped by the prayers and good works of the faithful. The Church embraces thus, in her divine and magnificent unity, Christians of all times and conditions. The charity which unites and shares all their spiritual goods is not confined to the living only, it reaches beyond the grave, to those who die in the peace of the Lord. For Charity, as St. Paul says, is not like Faith and Hope which cease with our last breath, it survives death and never perishes: *Charitas nunquam excidit.* Thus it is that the just after their death are not separated from the Church, nor cut off from the Communion of the Saints. They are always our brothers and friends. Like the angels and the blessed in heaven, we also can deliver the poor souls from their terrible prison. We can do even more; for the angels and saints can only help them with their prayers, whereas we can assist them by all kinds of suffrages and good works. God has given us, says Father Faber, such power over the fate of these poor souls that it would appear they depend upon earth more than upon Heaven. Such is the consoling doctrine of the Church,—such the touching belief in the Communion of Saints!

What joy and happiness must it not be to you, Christian and afflicted soul, who mourn a father, a mother, a husband, or cherished child! be comforted, you can still give them proofs of your love and attachment: you can be to them a delivering angel. Hasten then; come and break their chains; come and pay their debts, so that these dear souls may be received into the bosom of the Church Triumphant.

Second Point.—Not only is it in our power to assist, but it is our duty to help these unhappy souls. We owe it to God, the good and tender Father who loves them as his cherished spouses, and desires to open to them the gates of heaven, but his justice will not allow it. Then it is that He turns to us to make satisfaction for them; He gives us the means, and regards as done to Himself what we do for the most guilty and suffering of these souls. We then owe assistance to these poor exiles. Some amongst them, perhaps even a great many, suffer in Purgatory owing to our fault, to our negligence, to our bad advice, to our scandals. And shall we do nothing to relieve them? Shall we dare to say: "I am innocent of the tears of blood shed by these just souls." Finally, we owe it to ourselves. Let us not forget that we shall one day need, and perhaps soon, that the holy souls should exercise towards us the charity that we have now in our power to show them. According to St. Ambrose, all that piety inspires us to do for the dead will be changed into meritorious works for us, and, at the close of life, we shall receive a hundredfold all that we have given.

Christian soul, enter into yourself and question your conscience. Have you until now understood and practiced this important duty? Do you often think, and do you think daily of the suffering souls in Purgatory? Alas, what well-merited reproaches might they not have the right to address to you! Exercise towards them, in future, this charity that God commands and blesses; this charity which opens heaven both to him who practices it, and to him who is the object of it; this charity is the Christian's passport to the next world.

EXAMPLE

St. Catharine of Cortona, born of a noble family, was, when quite a child, distinguished for her fervent and angelic piety. Her father, who died before she had attained the age of eight years, appeared to her one day surrounded by the flames of Purgatory. "My daughter," said he, "I shall be detained in these flames until you shall have done penance for me." Catharine's heart was filled with compassion, and from that day she determined, young as she was, to undertake the wonderful austerities which made her so conspicuous for the extraordinary penances which she performed. Her tears, her prayers, and the mortifications she practiced soon paid the debt her father owed to Divine Justice, and, resplendent with heavenly light he again appeared to her and spoke to her in these words:

"God has accepted your suffrages and the satisfactory works you have offered, O my daughter; and I am now going to enjoy eternal glory. Continue during your whole life to immolate yourself as a victim for the salvation of the suffering souls. Such is the will of God."

The heroic virgin was faithful to her sublime mission, and all her life she prayed for and practiced untold austerities for the relief of the souls of the dead. When her pious companions tried to persuade her to lessen in some degree her penances, she answered them in these remarkable words, which reveal her life's secret:

"When one has seen, as I have seen, What Purgatory and hell are, one cannot do too much to deliver souls from the one, and preserve them from the other. I cannot then spare myself, as I offered myself as a sacrifice for them."

And we also, we have a duty and a mission to fulfill, which is to help the souls redeemed by Jesus Christ. Oh let us never be unmindful of it.

PRAYER

O God, mayest Thou be forever blest for having confided to me the relief of the souls Thou lovest and who have so many titles to my compassion. How consoling is it to me to have it in my power to wipe away their tears and open heaven to them. Recall often to my remembrance this great duty of charity, and help me to fulfill it. O Jesus, be merciful to our dear departed ones. Call thy children and our brethren to eternal bliss and may perpetual light shine upon them. May they rest in peace — *Requiescant in pace.*

FIFTEENTH DAY

THE FORGETFULNESS OF THE DEAD

I. It shows great unkindness.
II. It shows great ingratitude.

First Point.—It is related in the Gospel that a poor man, named Lazarus, lay covered with sores at the gate of a certain rich man. He asked but little, only for the crumbs which fell from the rich man's table, but these were refused him. Can we be surprised, that when the rich man died, he was, as Scripture tells us, buried in hell, whilst Lazarus was carried by the angels into Abraham's bosom.

The remembrance of our departed relatives is constantly before our hearts and minds. The house we live in, the name we bear, the worldly goods we have the use of, everything recalls them to our recollection. We do not really hear their voices crying out to us, their graves are silent, but the Church, our common mother, repeats to us without ceasing: "Have pity on your dead, for the hand of God has fallen upon them. Let some crumbs fall from your table to appease their hunger, some drops of water to quench their thirst." "*Thou wicked servant, . . . shouldst not thou, then, have had compassion on thy fellow-servant?*"—Matt. xviii. 32,33. After laboring and living for you all their lives, now that they ask for some crumbs of the inheritance they have left you, you refuse to give them anything. Oh! is not this great inhumanity? Christian soul, if, like the rich man in the Gospel, we are insensible to the cries of distress of our suffering brethren, will God hearken to ours? Will He receive us into his bosom? If He does not hurl us into hell, as He did the rich man, will He not condemn us for long years to the cleansing flames of Purgatory?

Second Point.—One of Pharaoh's officers, having incurred the displeasure of the king, was thrown with Joseph into prison. This latter was a man full of kind and compassionate feelings, and, becoming friends with his companion in misfortune, he endeavored to comfort him by interpreting his dreams, and giving him the assurance of a speedy deliverance. For the services he rendered him, the only return he asked was that he would remember him to the king; but, alas! the ungrateful wretch, elated with prosperity, forgot his benefactor, and the unfortunate Joseph was left to languish two years longer in his prison.

Christian soul, is not your heart moved with indignation at the recital of such cruel forgetfulness, but see if it does not meet its parallel in your own forgetfulness of your relatives and many benefactors—of those to whom you are indebted for your life, of those whose worldly goods you possess, and to whom you owe your fortune and position in life. Not long since, when they bid you a last farewell, and entreated you not to forget them, you replied, weeping: "What! I forget you? Oh, never, never! I would rather die myself than forget you!" But, alas! time has dried your tears, and already have you forgotten your dead. You no longer feel either regrets, or affection, or gratitude. You enjoy, as Pharaoh's officer did, the worldly goods they had acquired for you by the sweat of their brows, and you leave them to suffer, like Joseph, in the prison of Purgatory. Where, then, O Christian soul, is your faith, your conscience, your heart, your memory? O Lord God, make amends to them for this culpable forgetfulness, and give to our suffering and abandoned relatives eternal repose and glory.

EXAMPLE

Chaganus, having put to flight the army of Mauritius, exacted from the Emperor a large sum of money for the ransom of the many prisoners he had made. Mauritius refused. The conqueror then asked a less heavy sum, but this was likewise refused. Having reduced the amount of the required ransom to a mere nominal sum, without still being able to obtain it, the irritated barbarian gave orders to behead all the soldiers of the imperial army who were then in his power. But, what was the consequence? A few days after, Mauritius had a frightful vision. He found himself cited before the tribunal of God, and he saw a vast multitude of slaves in heavy chains. These unhappy wretches in dreadful words cried for vengeance on him. The Sovereign Judge, in an angry tone, said to Mauritius:

"Which would you prefer—to be punished in this world or in the next?"

"Lord," replied the terrified Emperor, "I prefer to be chastised in this world."

"In punishment, then, of your cruelty to these poor soldiers, whose lives you would not spare when you could have done it at so slight a cost, one of your soldiers shall take from you your crown, your reputation, and your life, and all your family shall share in your fall."

A few days after, the army mutinied and proclaimed Phocas emperor. Mauritius tried to escape in a small boat, but it was in vain. The adherents of Phocas seized him, loaded him with chains, and the unhappy father had the grief to see his five sons massacred before his eyes, and he himself died an ignominious death.

Christian soul, who hearest this fact of history, reflect that it is no longer a question of poor soldiers, but of your own brethren, of your dear relatives, who are the suffering prisoners of Divine Justice. God, who is all-merciful, asks you for this ransom, a prayer, a communion, an alms, a tear, and will you be so hard-hearted, so unfeeling as to refuse?

PRAYER

How can I, O Lord, forget the souls to whom Thou hast united me by the ties of affection and relationship. How can I abandon to their cruel sufferings those loved ones who, when alive, gave me such numberless proofs of tender and devoted affection? Every day of my life, even to my last breath, I am resolved to pray for them. O Jesus, be merciful to them! Call Thy children and our brethren to Thy Holy City, and may they eternally rest in peace! *Requiescant in pace.*

SIXTEENTH DAY

FIRST MOTIVE FOR SUCCORING THE SOULS IN PURGATORY: THE GLORY OF GOD

I. This devotion gives glory to God.
II. This devotion rejoices the Saints.

First Point.—The first motive which ought to induce us to hasten by every possible means the deliverance of the holy souls in Purgatory, is the glory that it gives to God. In effect, nothing glorifies the Most High, nothing makes his name more blessed, nothing pleases more his paternal heart, and nothing contributes more to the accomplishment of his adorable will than relieving the souls of the dead. Let us thoroughly understand that in opening heaven to them we give God more voices to praise Him, and more hearts to love and bless Him. We give Him souls, who at the foot of his eternal throne will be united to him with a love so pure, so perfect, so great, that it is not given to us to understand in this our land of exile. St. Augustine says that there is nothing more

77

pleasing to God than the relief and deliverance of the faithful departed, and Bourdaloue adds: "It is a more glorious, a greater and more meritorious apostleship than the conversion of sinners and infidels."

Let us, then, hasten to satisfy the demands of Divine Justice, and procure this glory for the suffering souls. They will, in return, do for us in heaven what we so imperfectly do on earth. Their pure and angelic voices will chant for us the canticle of our heavenly country which we cannot sing in a land of exile. By their songs of triumph we shall glorify the God of all glory and majesty, and God, who has promised that a glass of cold water, given in his name to a poor person, shall not go without its reward, will shower down his blessings on those who strive to unite to Him the souls He loves so tenderly.

Second Point.—Let us not forget that in delivering the holy souls by our prayers and suffrages, we not only glorify God but we give joy to the entire court of heaven. The entrance of another of the elect to the heavenly country is a family festival for its blessed inmates; all welcome and felicitate with fraternal joy the happy soul. Mary, the Mother of Mercy, the Consoler of the Church Suffering, rejoices with a holy joy, and with Jesus places on its brow the crown of glory and immortality promised to those who conquer. Its guardian angel and its patron saint hail it with ineffable joy and congratulate it on its deliverance and happiness. All the celestial court, which rejoices at the conversion of one sinner, rejoices still more in seeing the number of the elect increased, and intones new hymns to the glory of the Divine Lamb, whose grace, victorious over human weakness, raises the children of Adam to the throne of the fallen angels.

Christian soul, let us become attached to a devotion so pleasing to God and to all the friends of God. Let us listen no longer to the lamentations of the souls in Purgatory, but to the pressing invitations of Jesus Christ, of the Blessed Virgin and the saints, who supplicate us to free the unfortunate souls who weep in the horrible prison of Purgatory and to introduce them into the City of Bliss. Oh, let us restore these orphans to their Father in heaven, these poor exiles to their eternal country. One day, and it may be soon, we shall join them and partake of their happiness.

EXAMPLE

It is related in the Book of Daniel, that Darius, King of Persia, had passed a law, which, if broken, condemned the offender to be devoured by lions. The Prophet Daniel, who adored the one true God, being unable to observe the pagan law, was accused of not obeying the royal command. The king loved Daniel and was grieved to hear that he was accused of a crime that condemned him to be thrown into the lions' den; but, before letting him go, he said to him:

"Daniel, servant of God, fear not. What I cannot do without injury to my justice, I feel confident that the God you adore will do for you, and that He in his mercy will deliver you."

And so it came to pass. God watched miraculously over Daniel. He first closed the jaws of the lions, who instead of being his executioners, became his guardians, and then He sent an angel with food for him to eat.

This Scriptural narration is an emblem of what happens to the souls in Purgatory. God, when He sees them stained with sin and in debt to his Divine Justice, is unable to admit them into his kingdom; He is obliged to condemn them to the prison of expiation, and He says to them: "Go, but go with confidence; for what I myself am unable to do on account of my justice, another God will do for you, a God whom I myself have assigned to you. and who will be the minister of my mercies." And who is this God? No other than yourself, Christian soul. You are constituted the God of Purgatory, the same as Moses was placed as God over Egypt, and it is for you to relieve and deliver these poor prisoners; it is for you to take them the spiritual food which they so impatiently expect. Oh, is not this a noble and holy mission?

PRAYER

O God, infinitely good and loving, forget, I beseech Thee, the claims of Thy justice, to remember only those of Thy mercy; exercise it to its full extent towards the souls which are so dear to Thee. Receive them into Thy bosom and permit them to glorify Thee in heaven by their thanksgivings and eternal praises. Holy Mary, saints of God, intercede for them. Oh, Jesus be merciful to them, show them Thy face in the heavenly Jerusalem. May they rest in peace.—*Requiescant in pace.*

SEVENTEENTH DAY

SECOND MOTIVE FOR RELIEVING THE SOULS IN PURGATORY: THE LOVE OF OUR LORD

I. How much He loves the souls in Purgatory.
II. How much He desires that we should relieve them.

First Point.—Consider that Jesus Christ has an infinite love for the souls in Purgatory, the same as for all souls redeemed by the price of his blood. Each one may repeat with the great Apostle: "*He loved me, and delivered Himself for me*" (Galat. 2:20). If we are allowed to say that there are degrees in the infinite, Jesus ought to love them more than He loves us; because, confirmed in grace, incapable of sinning, they can never more offend Him; because they suffer greatly and with perfect resignation; and because they love Him more tenderly than we do. Yes, we cannot doubt but that the eyes and heart of the merciful Jesus are fixed upon our deceased brethren, upon these martyrs beyond the grave. Far from forgetting or abandoning them in their sufferings, it might be said that

He, as it were, suffers in them. Yes, He suffers as the Redeemer in these souls which He has purchased with so many sacrifices; as a Father, as a Spouse, as the Head of the members of his mystic body. Their sufferings remind Him of his sufferings, their love recalls his love. If He could die. He would die again to pay their debts and open to them the gates of heaven, and to restrain the force of his love it requires all the wisdom and merciful justice of a God who has a horror of the least stain of sin.

Christian soul, let us be animated by these same feelings of the heart of Jesus. Like Him let us love our brethren of the Church Suffering; let us love them tenderly on account of their sanctity and of the excess and duration of their sufferings; let us love them for the love of God as we love ourselves. Then it will come to pass that we shall feel deeply for them in their trials and we shall spare nothing for their relief.

Second Point.—Jesus cannot, Himself, deliver the souls in Purgatory; for Divine Justice forbids it. But, in the tabernacle, where love keeps Him a prisoner, He inspires the faithful on earth to pray for them and obtain for them peace and relief in their place of expiation. Our Lord spoke one day to St. Gertrude and said, "Each time you deliver one of these prisoners it is as pleasing to me as though you redeemed me from captivity, and I shall know well how to reward you." On the altar, where Jesus immolates Himself, He wills not that his sacrifice should ever be offered without the priest and assistants remembering the Church Suffering; and this takes place at the Memento of the Dead. He unites all his merits, and those of the Blessed Virgin and of the saints, and He asks the faithful to come and draw plentifully from this treasury and discharge the debts of the captive souls. "Take pity on these souls who are dear to Me; give Me back my children; deliver them by prayer, the Holy Sacrifice, and indulgences; hasten, oh! hasten the hour when it will be given to Me to crown them with glory and inundate them with torrents of delight." To excite our charity He ceases not to repeat what he once said to his disciples when speaking to them of the poor: "*As long as you did it to one of these, my least brethren, you did it to me;*" and one day He will reward us as if it had been He Himself whom we had delivered.

Christian soul, is not this a powerful motive to excite our zeal for so great, so holy a work, and one that is so easy to perform. Too happy should we be to have it in our power to satisfy so easily the ardent desires of the heart of Jesus.

EXAMPLE

A pious lady, a native of Luxemburg, appeared, some time after her death, to a very virtuous young girl and asked her to help her with her prayers. Whenever the young girl went to church and received Holy Communion the soul of the deceased lady accompanied her under a human form, and at the Elevation of the Mass her face was lighted up with such un expression of divine love that she seemed like to a seraph. Out of the church she was never seen. The young girl, surprised at her appearing thus, asked the reason.

The soul replied with a deep sigh: "Oh! you little know what the suffering is to be far from God! no words can express it. I feel drawn to God with such an ardent desire and irresistible longing, that to be deprived of Him in punishment of my faults is such anguish, that in comparison to it the pain of the fire which surrounds me is a mere nothing. In order to lessen the intensity of this suffering our Lord has permitted me to come to this church and adore Him here on earth, whilst awaiting the much wished-for day when I shall possess Him in heaven. His presence even under the mystic veils penetrates me to such a degree that I feel I can live only for Him; what then will it be when I see Him face to face in heaven?" And the poor soul besought the young girl to hasten, by her prayers, this happy moment.

PRAYER

O Jesus, full of mercy and goodness, Thou, who hast so great a love for man, who justifies him by faith and glorifies him by grace, I beseech Thee by the virtue of the wound of thy sacred side, which on the cross was opened by the lance, deliver the dead from the fire of Purgatory and render them worthy of the glory of thy saints. Be merciful to them, O Jesus, call thy children and our brethren to eternal bliss. May they rest in peace.—*Requiescant in pace.*

EIGHTEENTH DAY

THIRD MOTIVE FOR RELIEVING THE SOULS IN PURGATORY: THE LOVE OF MARY

I. She consoles the souls in Purgatory.
II. She delivers them.

First Point.—The Blessed Virgin is not satisfied with encouraging and consoling her children on earth, she is also the comforter of those that justice and love retain in the place of expiation. What mother is there, who seeing her child fall into a burning brazier, and, having it in her power to save it, would not fly to its relief? And Mary, the most loving of mothers, would she remain unmindful of the tortures of her children immersed in the expiatory flames of divine justice? Oh! no; full of compassion, she is unceasingly occupied in relieving them. There is not a suffering in this dark prison but what she softens; not an hour passes that she does not pour on the avenging fire a refreshing rain: "Oh!" exclaimed St. Vincent Ferrer, "how good is Mary to these unfortunate captives who suffer in Purgatory." Through her intercession they experience every moment some relief. The

Blessed Virgin, appearing to St. Bridget, said: "I am the mother of all those who are in Purgatory, and all the sufferings inflicted on the departed for the expiation of their sins are alleviated through my prayers."

Truly happy, then, are the true children of Mary; for her protection extends over them not only in this world, but she seeks to console them in those unseen and, to us, unfelt tortures, which may aptly be called the sufferings beyond the grave. Oh! how consoling is this thought and what a happiness to have such grounds for hoping that the Blessed Virgin will assist us at our last hour, and that if we fall into the abyss of Purgatory she will come to visit and comfort us. What a powerful motive is not this to love her tenderly during life. O Mary! Mother of Mercy, Comforter of the Afflicted, save us and deliver us from Purgatory.

Second Point.—The most holy Virgin does not limit the assistance she gives the captive souls to visiting and relieving them, but, through her intercession, she delivers them. In order to hasten the end of their sufferings she inspires the living to help them by their suffrages, and she supplicates her Divine Son to admit them to the dwelling of peace. What Mary asks she always obtains, and if it were not that she hastened the hour of their deliverance, how many souls, forgotten by others or insufficiently helped, would suffer for long years the unutterable pains of Purgatory? And when the Church celebrates, in a special manner, her festivals, how many are there who then mount to heaven on the wings of her love. The learned and pious Gerson asserts, that on the day of her Assumption into heaven, all the souls detained in Purgatory were delivered through her intercession. It is also a pious belief, that this loving mother descends, on Saturdays and on her festival days, into the dungeons of Divine Justice and liberates many of the prisoners, whose pardon she has obtained, rejoicing to take her children with her into the abodes of bliss. Yes, in those realms, an untold multitude of the blessed owe their deliverance from Purgatory to the Queen of Heaven.

Christian soul, pray daily to Mary in favor of your dear departed ones, and ask of her their deliverance. For this end offer, from time to time, some acts of mortification, a Communion, and a visit to some chapel where she is more especially honored. Repeat often, "O compassionate mother, take pity on my suffering relatives, obtain for them eternal rest. Remember that they are thy children and thou their mother."

EXAMPLE

A holy Religious had, for a considerable length of time, bestowed much care on a poor girl who needed it much, both as regarded soul and body. Her conduct had given rise to much scandal, and, broken down in health, her temper was such, that none of the neighbors cared to go near her, or give her the assistance she required. The good Religious, alone, surmounting all natural feelings of repugnance, brought her food, and rendered her the services she needed; but, instead of showing gratitude for her kindness, the wretched girl repaid her with insolence. When the sister spoke to her of God, she answered with blasphemies.

One day a severe attack seized her, and she died almost suddenly. On the point of appearing before the Sovereign Judge, she remembered the mercies of Mary, whom in her youth she had been used to invoke, and, addressing her, said: "O thou who didst never abandon those whom all others had abandoned, Mother of Mercy, come to my assistance. If thou forsakest me I am lost." And Mary came and helped the sinner, inspiring such acts of repentance as saved her from hell.

Next day her corpse was found stretched on the ground, and all agreed that her soul must be lost. Even the good Sister felt so certain that such must be her fate, that she tried to banish the recollection of her from her thoughts. One day, however, the soul that she imagined lost was permitted by God to appear and speak to her.

"How is it," said she, "that you pray for everyone, and you forget me?"

"Is it possible," replied the Sister, "that you are in Purgatory?" And the poor sinner related the miracle which had been worked for her salvation when she was in her agony, and she implored the Sister to pray to the Blessed Virgin to deliver her from Purgatory, as she had delivered her from hell.

The Sister prayed fervently, and, after a time, she learned from a second apparition that her prayer had been heard, and that, through Mary's intercession, the gates of heaven had been opened to that penitent soul. Oh, how good and merciful is Mary!

PRAYER

Hail, Queen of Mercy! our life, our sweetness, and our hope, not only in this valley of tears, but also in the place of expiation. We cry to thee, Comfort of the Afflicted, weeping and mourning for our suffering brethren in Purgatory. Turn then, O Gracious Advocate, thy merciful eyes towards them; show unto them Jesus, the blessed fruit of thy womb. It is what we earnestly ask of thee, O clement, O pious Queen, O sweet Virgin Mary.—*Requiescant in pace.*

NINETEENTH DAY

FOURTH MOTIVE FOR ASSISTING THE SOULS IN PURGATORY: THE GRATITUDE OF THE DEAD

I. In Purgatory.
II. In Heaven.

First Point.—It is a generally received opinion amongst theologians that the suffering souls of the faithful departed can, even in Purgatory, intercede for those who help them. It is true that they cannot obtain anything for themselves, and their prayers are not heard when they petition for the end of their own sufferings, but it is otherwise when they offer their prayers for their benefactors. These latter supplications are in accordance with the designs of Providence; they have the necessary conditions, and are free from the defects which so often cause ours to be unheard. These souls are pure and holy, beloved by our Lord, and always perfectly united to Him; they pray without distractions, fervently and with perseverance, and their influence is so great, says a pious author, that were it not for daily experience we should hardly credit it.

We have, then, O Christian soul, everything to gain in the exchange of our prayers with those of our deceased brethren; and the most sure way of obtaining from God what we desire, is to make them take an interest in our cause by confiding it to them, and in offering for them our good works—the Holy Sacrifice of the Mass, and as many indulgences as we have it in our power to apply to them. Oh! let us pray often, let us pray much, for the blessed and grateful souls in Purgatory, and they will offer their efficacious prayers for us! They will offer for us to God all the merit of their ineffable sufferings. Oh! yes, the thought of the dead is, indeed, as Scripture says, a holy and wholesome thought. *Sancta cogitatio.*

Second Point.—There is no ingratitude in heaven, and the souls delivered by our suffrages will forever be united to us by ties of never-ending gratitude. Could they forget us, when it is we who have put them into the possession of eternal riches, and clothed them with the robe of glory and immortality; when it is we who have restored to them their places at the banquet of the Lamb, where they will eat the bread of angels, for which they hunger. Oh, no! they will certainly never forget us; they will think of us, they will be mindful of our wants, they will watch over us as so many guardian angels. From their high thrones they will look down on the perils and evils that beset us, they will incessantly beseech God to spare us trials, and remove far from us all temptations and dangers, and will unite their supplications to those we address to the most Sacred Heart. What a powerful assistance will they not be to us in our needs and alleviation in our troubles! What invaluable helpers during life, what supports and comforters in our last agony, what powerful advocates at the day of judgment! And, if we pass into Purgatory, the souls we shall have delivered, will not they, in their turn, come and visit and comfort us until the happy moment arrives when we join them in the splendors of eternal bliss.

How great are the advantages and what consolations of every kind does not devotion to the souls in Purgatory ensure. Happy, then, and most happy, are they who pray for the dead: "All that we give them through charity," says St. Ambrose, "is changed into graces for us, and after death we shall find the merit a hundredfold."

EXAMPLE

A pious person, whose word is not to be doubted, relates the following fact, as a proof of the efficacy of prayers for the souls in Purgatory:

"I was very anxious to recover my health, and, for this end, I had prayed to Our Lady of Lourdes, to the Infant Jesus, and to St. Joseph, but in vain—I obtained nothing. It was not until I had asked the Holy Souls to pray for me that my request was granted. I promised them, that if, by Christmas, I could fulfill all my religious duties, and resume my ordinary occupations, 1 would have Masses offered, and obtain many suffrages for them. May these dearly-loved intercessors be forever blessed. I am perfectly cured, and I hasten to do all that I had promised. From this fact we may see how much God desires the deliverance of the captive souls of Purgatory, since he obliges us, as it were. to have recourse to them, and to pray for them, in order to obtain the many graces that He wills to grant through their intercession. As for me, I am perfectly convinced of the truth of it, and can vouch, that for all the favors that God grants me, I am indebted to my good friends of Purgatory. All that I ask for, without having recourse to them, I do not obtain; but, in union with them, I never despair, I hope even against hope."

Learn by this example, O Christian soul, and be convinced that you can obtain all you wish through the mediation of our departed brethren.

PRAYER

O Holy Souls in Purgatory! I beseech the Lord Jesus, who died for you, to have pity on your sufferings. May He, through the shedding of his precious blood, grant you relief in your torments. And, in return, O charitable souls, intercede for me: your prayers will be heard, for you are in a state of grace. Ask, then, for me, the spiritual and temporal favors I need, and, above all, ask for me a holy death, and that, one day, I may be with you in heaven.—*Requiescant in pace.*

TWENTIETH DAY

THE FIRST MEANS FOR ASSISTING THE SOULS IN PURGATORY: PRAYER

I. An easy means.
II. An efficacious means.

First Point.—Having considered in the preceding chapters the motives which urge us to assist the holy souls in Purgatory, we must now examine what are the most efficacious means for helping them.

The first of these is prayer, which is within the reach of everyone—of the poor as of the rich, of the weak as of the strong, of the young as of the aged; no one can with reason plead to be dispensed. You do not like to mortify your body by fasts, you do not feel inclined to open your purse to give alms, you must, then, pray—oh! pray often for the departed; pray in the morning, pray in the evening, pray in the day, and pray even at night. Who is there who cannot give this alms of prayer, which relieves pain? Who does not find in his heart a supplication for the relief of these untold sufferings? Who is there amongst us who, mourning for his deceased relatives, cannot raise to God a heartfelt prayer? Is it possible that we should allow a friend or relative to suffer, who could be relieved by prayer, and we not offer it! This would not be indifference, but cruelty. To pray for our unfortunate brethren is not only easy, but sweet and consoling. It is so pleasing to converse and be occupied with those we love!

Christian soul, make a resolution never to let a day pass without praying for your dear deceased relatives. Offer for them the pain that you experience in prayer from distractions or dryness; or, at least, repeat often the short ejaculations: "*Sweet Jesus, be merciful to them! Eternal rest give to them, O Lord! May they rest in peace!*"

Second Point.—Prayer, according to St. Augustine, is the golden key which opens heaven: *Oratio clavis est cæli.* Powerful beyond all other means, it flows from the human heart, rises on the wings of angels and reaching to the throne of God, goes straight to his heart, touches it, softens it, and silences justice, so that love only can be heard. Vanquished by prayer, Divine Justice yields, relents, and pardons; then, armed with the sentence of pardon, prayer descends from the throne of God into the abyss, and there, leaning over the poor souls who await the hour of their deliverance, it extinguishes the avenging fire which burns them, and breaking forever the chains which hold them captive, restores them to liberty and happiness. This is what prayer for the dead can do. It admits of no obstacle, no distance or length of time affects it; heaven opens to it, the abyss closes beneath it; it obtains everything, it triumphs over everything. St. Thomas asserts that God receives more favorably prayers offered for the dead than those offered for the living.

The psalm *De Profundis* has been selected by the Church as a special prayer for the dead, and she engages us, by her example, to recite it often for this intention. The words of the psalm are eloquently expressive of the grief, the resignation, the love, the hope of the poor souls who burn in the depths of the abyss. Let us resolve to recite it often, or, at least, morning and night, at the end of our usual prayers.

EXAMPLE

When St. Monica was dying, she called her son, Augustine, to her bedside and said: "My son, I die happy, I have obtained from God what was the one wish of my life. Yes, I die happy.

My dear son, when I shall have breathed my last, forget not in your prayers, and forget not at the altar her who is doubly your mother. Remember always the soul of Monica."

Augustine, deeply affected, could reply only with his tears, and Monica expired in the joy of the Lord. During the twenty years that he survived his mother, Augustine never ceased to pray and offer the Holy Sacrifice of the Mass for the repose of her who had loved him so much. He went further. He begged all the priests of his acquaintance, and all who should read his books in future ages, to be mindful, at the altar, of his mother Monica; "so that," added he, "these numerous supplications may open heaven to her."

Let us, Christian soul, follow the example of St. Augustine and pray much for our dear deceased relatives; let us pray always and without ceasing for them. And if we have had the misfortune to lose our mother, let us never forget her.

PRAYER

Lord Jesus, who hast said, "*Ask, and you shall receive, seek, and you shall find, knock, and it shall be opened to you*" (Matt. 7:7), I beg and entreat, by the bowels of Thy divine mercy, to have pity on the poor souls who suffer in Purgatory. Reject not my prayers, sweet and loving Savior, hearken to my petitions and open to my friends and relatives the gates of the heavenly dwelling place. May they rest in eternal peace.—*Requiescant in pace.*

TWENTY-FIRST DAY

THE SECOND MEANS OF RELIEVING
THE SOULS IN PURGATORY: ALMS

I. Corporal alms.
II. Spiritual alms.

First Point.—To give alms is one of the virtues which the Gospel recommends the most frequently and the most strongly, and, according to St. Thomas, it possesses greater powers of satisfaction than prayer, or rather it doubles the power of prayer and ensures its success. The angel said to Tobias: "*Alms delivereth from death, and the same is that which purgeth away sins, and maketh to find mercy and life everlasting*" (Tobias, 12:9).

What more efficacious means for relieving the suffering souls than to practice, in their name, acts of charity. The grateful voices of the poor reach God, and near Him triumph over everything. It is like a gentle dew falling on the flames of Purgatory and mitigating their severity; and how consoling to think that the alms which gives bread to a poor person gives perhaps to a ransomed soul a place forever at the table of the Lord in heaven. Oh, let us, then, be as merciful as it is in our power to be; if we have much, let us give much; if we have little, let us give little, but let us give it willingly. "*Blessed is he,*" says the Psalmist, "*that understandeth concerning the needy and the poor; the Lord will deliver him in the evil day. The Lord help him on his bed of sorrow*" (Ps. 11:2,4).

Christian soul, relieve the poor in this world, for by so doing you relieve those beyond the grave. Place the widow's mite in the hand of the poor, they are the jailors of Purgatory, and, at the sound of their voices the fire will be extinguished, the dungeons will open, and the prisoners will regain their freedom.

Second Point.—Should it happen that we have not worldly goods nor money at our disposal, can we not at least give spiritual alms, which benefit the soul and heart of those who mourn and suffer, and which, according to St. Thomas, are as much superior to corporal alms as the spirit is superior to the body? Spiritual sufferings are more numerous. and more to be deplored than corporal sufferings. God, in his infinite goodness, allows us to transfer to the holy souls of Purgatory the merit that we could obtain by this kind of alms. For them, let us nurse the sick; for them let us watch beside the pillow of the dying; for them let us visit prisoners; for them let us protect orphans; for them let us comfort widows; for them let us dry the tears of those who mourn; so that our acts of charity, in lessening the sufferings of this life, which are a Purgatory, may at the same time mitigate and shorten, for our deceased brethren, the Purgatory of the next life.

What is there, then, to stop us when it is a question of the relief and deliverance of these beloved souls? What can excuse us if we forget them, when it is so easy for us to help them? And who will come to our assistance if we do nothing for others?

EXAMPLE

A widow had an only son, whom she loved tenderly. One day, when amusing himself with young companions of his own age, a stranger, passing that way, tried to annoy him. The widow's son spoke harshly to him, whereupon the stranger drew out his dagger, and, plunging it into his breast, left the unfortunate youth dying on the ground. With the bloody instrument of his crime still in his hand, the assassin fled, and took refuge in the first house that was open, beseeching the woman to whom it belonged, to hide him for the love of God, little knowing she was the mother of the young man he had murdered. The good woman consented, and the men who were in search of the culprit, not being able to find him, addressing her said:

"You are probably not aware that your son has been killed, for if you were you would denounce his murderer, who, we still think, may be here." The poor mother, on hearing the fatal news, nearly died of grief; but, after a time, her charity and courage returning, she said to the young man:

"Wretch, that you are, you have killed my son, who was the support of my old age, and my only hope. It is in my power to deliver you up to justice, and you will be put to death, but I prefer, through charity, to return good for evil. You may stay here: I will obtain your pardon, and adopt you, and I hope God will in return open Heaven to my dear son."

Some days later the deceased son appeared to his mother and said: "Wipe away your tears and be joyful, for you have saved me, I should have remained long in Purgatory, but you have delivered me by your generosity, and the charity you showed to him who deprived me of life. O, my mother, be comforted; I now ascend to Heaven." How true it is that charity is all powerful.

PRAYER

With a firm belief in Thy Word, O my Savior, I will henceforth see only Thy adorable person in the poor when they ask for help. I will place my alms in the hand held out to me, thinking that it is to Thee I give. But my charity shall not be shown to the living only—it shall extend to the dead; and what I do for the poor of this world shall benefit the poor of Purgatory, and draw down upon them the fullness of Thy mercy. Sweet Jesus, grant them eternal rest!—*Requiescant in pace.*

TWENTY-SECOND DAY

THE THIRD MEANS OF RELIEVING THE SOULS IN PURGATORY: HOLY COMMUNION

I. Sacramental Communion.
II. Spiritual Communion.

First Point.—When we have the happiness to receive Communion, we are so intimately united to Jesus Christ, that we may exclaim, with the great Apostle, "*I live, now; not I, but Christ liveth in me.*" Our flesh becomes his flesh, his heart makes ours vibrate, his blood flows in our veins, his divinity resides in us: We are so many Christs! At this happy moment, which the angels envy, how easy is it for us to speak to God without the sound of words, and say to Him, with greater confidence than the Royal Prophet: "Behold, O God, our protector, and look on the face of Thy Christ." *Respice in faciem Christi Tui.* No; it is no longer I who speak and pray, it is Jesus, Thy own Son, who speaks and prays for me; it is He who, in my place, asks for the deliverance of my father, of my mother, for the deliverance of the poor abandoned souls. Oh, merciful Father, I feel confident Thou wilt not reject these just supplications, for the prayers, the tears, the blood of Jesus Christ have an all-powerful voice to appease justice and obtain pardon.

Communicate then, O Christian soul, and communicate often for these loved ones who have no longer the happiness of participating in the Eucharistic banquet. Oh, with what eagerness, and with what holy impatience do they wait for us to bestow on them the refreshing and liberating dew of the blood of Christ! Soon, and how consoling is the thought, soon the never-ending communion will begin for them, and they will contemplate, in heaven, the Eucharistic Savior, who is become the God who rewards.

Second Point.—If, Christian soul, it is not in your power to receive Sacramental Communion frequently, make at least Spiritual Communions, which consist in an ardent desire to be united to the Divine Savior, and to receive his spirit and graces. This practice is so beneficial to both the living and the dead, that St. Liguori goes so far as to say, that as much or even more fruit can be obtained by it, than by tepid Sacramental Communions. It possesses, besides, the advantage that it can be made every day, and at any time of the day or night, and in every place, whether holy or profane. Is not this a simple, easy, and powerful means to assist our dear departed ones?

Christian soul, endeavor to make this Spiritual Communion at least when you hear Mass, and each time you visit the Blessed Sacrament. An easy method is the following:—"My Jesus, I believe Thee here present; I love Thee, I long for Thee, I unite myself to Thee in spirit and affection, until I shall have the happiness of receiving Thee in reality. Bless me, and bless also the poor suffering souls in Purgatory. O Lord God, call Thy children and our brethren to eternal rest, and may perpetual light shine on them. May they rest in peace.—*Requiem æternam dona eis Domine!*

EXAMPLE

The venerable Blosius, well known as a great authority on spiritual matters, and a man remarkable for wisdom, relates that a devout servant of God, with whom he was intimately acquainted, was visited by a soul in Purgatory, who made known to him all the torments it was suffering, in punishment for having received Holy Communion with lukewarmness, and but little preparation.

On this account, it was condemned by Divine Justice to the torment of a consuming fire. "I entreat you," said the soul, "you who were my intimate and faithful friend, and who ought still to be the same, I entreat you to receive Communion in my name, with all the love and fervor you possibly can, and I feel confident that this fervent Communion will suffice for my deliverance, and atone for the tepidity I was guilty of."

The friend hastened to hear Mass, and communicate devoutly for the repose of his unhappy friend. Having made his act of thanksgiving, the soul appeared again, surrounded by dazzling brightness, and, with gratitude said:

"May you be blessed, kindest of friends, your Communion has delivered my soul, and I am going to see my adorable Master face to face."

This example should remind us of the advice of St. Bonaventure: "Let charity induce you to communicate often and devoutly, for there is nothing which is more efficacious for the eternal repose of the dead."

PRAYER

O my God, the souls of my relatives are detained in the prison of Thy justice, but by receiving the Bread of Angels, I can open the gates for them. I bless thee, O merciful Father, deign to receive the promise I this day make, to communicate often, and fervently, for the holy souls in Purgatory, so that Thou mayest see in me only Thy Son, that He may speak in me; and thus I may obtain with greater certainty the grace I ask. O Jesus, show mercy to our dear departed, and may they rest in peace. —*Requiescant in pace.*

TWENTY-THIRD DAY

FOURTH MEANS OF ASSISTING THE SOULS IN PURGATORY: THE HOLY SACRIFICE OF THE MASS

I. It is offered by Jesus Christ.
II. We offer it with Him.

First Point.—No means, amongst the many already named for relieving the souls in Purgatory, is as powerful and as efficacious as the Holy Sacrifice of the Mass, which is a most consoling article of faith. The reason is, that all the efficacy of the Divine Sacrifice arises from its being offered in the person and in the name of Jesus Christ. On the Altar, as on Calvary, the Victim is the same—the same High Priest and, consequently, the same efficacy. Jesus, in the Blessed Sacrament, offers to his Father all that He is and all that He has. He offers all the members of the Church Militant and of the Church Suffering. What joy is there in this land of tears, when Jesus, as it were, embraces these souls—victims of Divine Justice,—and offers them all to his Father! And the Father receives the oblation of the Son; He recognizes, through the expiatory flames, the features of this adorable Son that are stamped upon them even in their disgrace, and He pardons, in consideration of this spotless Lamb. How is it then that, at so solemn a moment, all these souls are not delivered? We know not, we cannot penetrate the secrets of the infinite justice and the holiness of God, but it is certain that all receive some relief. A holy Doctor of the Church even affirms that, every day, after each Mass, many of the captive souls leave Purgatory and take their flight to Heaven. In a Convent at Rome there is a painting representing St. Bernard saying Mass, and souls leaving Purgatory, ascending gradually to Heaven as the Mass continued. How is it that we so seldom think of these wonderful things?

In many Catholic families a custom prevails of having a solemn Mass celebrated for deceased relatives and friends, not only at the time of death, but at the end of every year. Have you, Christian soul, fulfilled this pious duty; have you had an anniversary Mass said for your father, your mother, your brother, and your sister? Omit it not in future; have pity on them. *Miseremini.*

Second Point.—If your means do not allow you to have Masses offered often for your private intentions, do not forget, Christian soul, that you can offer it in a certain way yourself, that is, by devoutly uniting your prayers to those of our Lord. Yes; when you are there near the altar, you can dispose of the merits of the spotless Lamb; you can apply them to those who are dear to you, and as Mary and Joseph guided the steps and actions of the Infant God, you can exercise authority over Jesus in the Eucharist. You become the master and the dispenser of his merits. You can take his Sacred Blood, and shed it with profusion on the holy souls in Purgatory. You can apply the fruit of the sacrifice to them, that is, the part to which you are entitled, of all the Masses that are said in the world. This is, indeed, an immense treasure, of which we do not think sufficiently; for with it we can pay the ransom of our relatives and friends who mourn in the sad dwelling-place of their captivity, and open for them the gates of heaven.

Alas! how guilty shall we be if we neglect so easy and efficacious a means of putting an end to the sufferings of these dear souls, who ask us through the bowels of compassion of the Savior, to remember them, often during Mass at the "Memento of the Dead."

EXAMPLE

The venerable Curé of Ars used to assure his hearers that one Mass was of more value than all good works put together, for the latter are the works of man, whereas the Sacrifice of the Mass is the work of God. It is related by a pious author that a very holy monk was one day offering up Mass for the souls in Purgatory. When he had pronounced the words, "Lamb of God, who takest away the sins of the world, give them rest," he heard a multitude of distant voices calling out: "Make haste, make haste, come and receive rest, for the Mass will soon be ended;" and at the time of Communion, whilst he held the body of Jesus Christ in his hands, he was rapt in ecstasy, and saw a crowd of souls hastening to receive rest. And as they retired after receiving it others called out: "Hasten, hasten, for Mass is about to end."

Thus the monk remained standing at the altar from early morning to nine o'clock, when he finished Mass, and his Superior obliged him under obedience to tell the rest of the community of his ecstasy, and the vision he had had.

PRAYER

O merciful God, however guilty the souls in Purgatory are, Thou wilt pardon them at the sight of the Precious Blood of thy Son shed every day on the altar to blot out their iniquities. Yes, Thou wilt hear the voice of this Adorable Blood, which asks not vengeance, but mercy and pardon. O Jesus! spotless Lamb, who takest away the sins of the world, be merciful to my departed brethren, that they may be delivered from captivity, and repose near Thee in peace.—*Requiescant in pace.*

TWENTY-FOURTH DAY

FIFTH MEANS OF RELIEVING THE SOULS IN PURGATORY: SUFFERING

I. Voluntary suffering.
II. Involuntary suffering.

First Point.—"Let us relieve the souls in Purgatory," says St. John Chrysostom; "let us relieve them by everything that is a pain to us, for God is mindful to apply the merits of the living to the dead. Suffering is the great satisfaction that the Lord asks of their love in order to appease his justice; let us, then, suffer for them, so that they may suffer less. Oh! if we had a more lively faith and a more ardent charity, what acts of mortification should we not impose upon ourselves so as to relieve and deliver relatives and friends who loved us so much, and who now suffer in such a terrible manner. Penitential works, fasts, and other austerities would then form a part of our daily actions. At all events, let us have the courage to offer some little sacrifices; the sacrifice of a pleasure, the sacrifice of a dangerous affection, the sacrifice of a bad book, the sacrifice of an habitual fault, the sacrifice of some object of luxury and vanity. "Choose," said Father Felix, "the best victim, and choose it more especially in the depths of your heart. Sacrifice what is dearest to you for those whom you love best; sacrifice yourself, and let the price of this personal sacrifice be the ransom for those who suffer."

"With the eyes of faith we shall see these holy souls raised to heaven on the wings of our sacrifices, austerities, and sufferings. They go triumphantly, thanking us for our generosity, and when they enter into glory they will repay us with superabundance for all that we shall have done for them. What a subject for consolation and hope! O God, O crucified Jesus, make us understand the price of suffering.

Second Point.—If, however, we have not courage for voluntary suffering, Providence inflicts sufferings which are more meritorious both for us and for the dead, because they are not of our choice. These consist of pains of the soul and of the body which are inevitable in this world. Alas! we know it too well, they are found everywhere, in every station, and under every condition. Our life on earth is a daily combat, a long and painful martyrdom; ought we to complain of it? Oh no, since all our sufferings can become a means of salvation for us and for others; since we can make use of them to relieve the most cruel of all pains, that which is undergone by the holy souls in Purgatory. Yes; with this cross that Providence places on our shoulders, with this thorn which tears our heart, with a tear, a sigh, with an act of resignation we can alleviate the great sufferings beyond the grave and dry the tears of our loved relatives.

Let us then take courage, O Christian soul; let us bear a little cold, for by that means we shall refresh the victims who burn in the midst of fire kindled by the anger of God. Let us bear a little heat, for we shall by that means change the heat of that fire into a refreshing dew. Let us bear any little discomfort, for by that means we shall snatch souls from the depths of the abyss. Let us accept fatigue and lassitude, for by that means we shall raise them to thrones of glory in heaven. To us a momentary suffering; to them an eternity of happiness!

EXAMPLE

St. Antoninus relates that a sick person besought God with many tears to free him from his excruciating sufferings. An angel appeared to him and said, "The Lord sends me to you to give you your choice, a year of suffering on earth or a single day in Purgatory." The sick man did not hesitate. "One day in Purgatory," said he, "and I shall at least see the end of my sufferings." He expired soon after, and his soul was precipitated into the abyss of expiation.

Then the compassionate angel came to comfort him. On seeing him the unfortunate man uttered a terrible cry, that was like a shriek from hell, and called out: "Deceitful angel, you have deceived me; you assured me that I should be but a single day in Purgatory, and already I have passed twenty years in the most frightful torments."

"Unfortunate soul," replied the angel, "you are mistaken; the severity of your torments has made you exaggerate the length of time, and caused you to imagine an age what is but the effect of a moment. Be not deceived; your death took place but a few minutes ago, and your corpse is not yet cold."

"Obtain, then leave for me to return to earth, to suffer for a year all that God pleases." His request was granted, and the sick man endeavored to induce those who came to see him to accept willingly all the pains of this world, rather than expose themselves to the torments of the next. He often repeated:

"Patience in suffering is the golden key of heaven." Let us, then, profit by the sufferings Providence is pleased to send us, both for ourselves and for the souls in Purgatory.

PRAYER

Blessed be Thou, O God, who willest that the pains and constant sufferings which embitter my life, should become to me an abundant source of merit, giving me thus the means of satisfying Thy justice for the souls which are so dear to me. From henceforth, instead of complaining of the heaviness of my cross, I will carry it with patience and resignation, and Thou wilt cast on my deceased relatives a look of mercy. O Jesus, be merciful to them; call thy children and our brethren to Thee, and may they rest in peace.—*Requiescant in pace.*

TWENTY-FIFTH DAY

SIXTH MEANS OF RELIEVING THE SOULS IN PURGATORY: THE WAY OF THE CROSS

I. It is the way to heaven for the living.
II. It is the way to heaven for the dead.

First Point.—Consider that this devotion so venerable on account of the holiness of its origin, so great on account of the recollections it awakens, and so precious on account of the advantages it procures, is the most efficacious means for conquering our passions and the most certain path for reaching speedily the summit of perfection. The horror of sin which caused Jesus Christ such agony: the fear of committing it, so as not to renew the sufferings of His passion; a spirit of self-sacrifice and penance, in imitation of Him; zeal for the salvation of souls who have cost Him so dear; love of humility and abjection; pardon of injuries, contempt of the world, patience in the trials of life, self-renunciation; all these things we find at every step of the way of sorrows. Can there be anything more instructive, more consoling, and more edifying? "If," says St. Bonaventure, "you wish to advance from virtue to virtue, to draw down upon yourself grace upon grace, and become like, not only to the angels but to God Himself, practice frequently this pious exercise." O holy Way of the Cross, you shall always be to me a delight and the royal way which conducts to heaven!

Christian soul, do you desire, according to the recommendation of the Apostle to "be justified still," and to "be sanctified still?" (Apoc. 22:11). No shorter or more sure method can be pointed out to advance in virtue and "be made conformable to the image of His Son" (Rom. 8:29), than to study thus the divine example which is shown to us on the way to Calvary. Yes, make often the Stations of the Cross, following the example of the Blessed Virgin, of the first disciples of our Lord, and of a multitude of holy persons, and each time you will feel yourself better, more devout, and nearer to heaven.

Second Point.—The way of the Cross is also a most salutary practice for our dear departed friends and relatives. Following our crucified Lord on the sorrowful way to Calvary we collect each drop of His precious blood, each merit of His painful martyrdom, and we offer them to the justice of God, to pay the debts of the imprisoned souls. At each Station we can fancy that we hear a sound from beyond the grave; a sound of joy and relief. This holy exercise is, moreover, salutary to the dead, on account of the many indulgences attached to it, and which are applicable to them. These indulgences are so numerous that, according to Benedict XIV, they cannot be enumerated; to gain them it suffices to be in a state of grace—Confession and Communion not being enjoined. This devotion may be repeated several times the same day.

If then you desire to relieve and deliver many souls in Purgatory, make the Stations of the Cross. You will find on this sorrowful way, consecrated by the sufferings and death of Jesus Christ, the consolation your heart needs to enable it to bear the loss of those you still mourn, and it will be the means of opening heaven to them. Resolve henceforth to make the Stations of the Cross every Friday, that memorable day which has so many claims on our gratitude.

EXAMPLE

St. Mary Magdalen of Pazzi, animated by feelings of great charity and affection, attended the deathbed of a Sister of her Order, who during life had been greatly esteemed by the community. The Religious hastened not only to recite the Divine Office for her, but they also offered all the indulgences they were able to gain in the course of the day. The corpse of the deceased Sister was still exposed in the Church, and St. Mary Magdalen, who was at the grate praying for the repose of her soul, kept looking at it with affection, when, suddenly, the soul of the departed, surrounded with dazzling light seemed to issue from the inanimate remains, and rising up, ascended to heaven to receive the crown of immortality. At the same time our Lord appeared to the saint, and told her that the reason this soul had been so speedily delivered from Purgatory was through the efficacy of the indulgences which had been offered for her. Ever after this event, so great was the devotion of the Religious of the monastery to indulgences that they were most particular never to omit the gaining of all those in their power.

Let us imitate their example and never let an opportunity pass of gaining indulgences for the poor souls in Purgatory, especially those of the Stations of the Cross. By practicing this devotion the same indulgences can be gained as are granted to those who visit the sacred places of Jerusalem.

PRAYER

O Mary, Mother of Sorrows! thou who didst so often meditate on the mystery of the Passion of thy Divine Son, thou who wert the first to visit those places consecrated by His sufferings, teach as to meditate and practice, like thee, this holy and salutary devotion. Grant that by it we may find the grace of conversion for sinners, of perseverance for the just, and consolation for the souls in Purgatory. Sweet Jesus, give to these blessed souls eternal rest.—*Requiescant in pace.*

TWENTY-SIXTH DAY

SEVENTH MEANS FOR RELIEVING THE SOULS IN PURGATORY INDULGENCES

I. How precious they are.
II. How they can be gained.

First Point.—Our sins are so numerous and so great and our satisfaction so slight, that it would be difficult to discharge the temporal debt due for our sins if the Church did not supplement our weakness by opening to us the treasury of indulgences. This is an immense and inexhaustible treasury, which contains the superabundant merits of our Lord Jesus Christ, of the Blessed Virgin and the Saints, the key of which is entrusted to the Sovereign Pontiff. Nothing is more beneficial to the living or dead, after the Sacrifice of the Mass and Holy Communion than indulgences; they may be said to be the last effort of Divine Mercy for the salvation of souls. By means of indulgences, which are so numerous, so easy to gain, and within reach of everyone, we are able to satisfy Divine Justice and redeem the souls who are dear to us, and who are expiating in flames the faults and errors of their past lives. We can compare these numerous indulgences, which the Church bestows so liberally, to a miraculous rain, which refreshes those who thirst, consoles those who weep, and procures the beatific joy of those who are in captivity. Truly this treasure is an admirable and fatherly invention.

Christian soul, let us then hasten to acquire these spiritual riches, more precious than gold, and never more abundant and numerous than at the present day. Let us endeavor to gain them frequently, and as many of them as possible, saying to ourselves: I will gain this indulgence for my beloved parents, for such a relative, for such a friend, for the most abandoned soul, for the soul which suffers most. I will help these souls that I love and weep for.

Second Point.—Three conditions are requisite for gaining indulgences. First, it is necessary to be in a state of grace. God wills that before helping others, we should close hell beneath our own feet; besides, we must remember that all works performed when in a state of mortal sin, are dead works and devoid of merit. Secondly, it is necessary to have at least a general intention of gaining indulgences, and for this end it is advisable to renew every day in morning prayer the intention of gaining all the indulgences attached to the different pious practices that are performed during the course of the day. Thirdly, all the conditions prescribed must be faithfully fulfilled. In general, these conditions consist of acts that are very easy to perform, which require but little time, and are within everyone's capacity, such as a short prayer, a small alms, an act of mortification, or a communion.

Christian soul, for pity's sake, never neglect to procure for the faithful departed those treasures which can so easily be gained. Carelessness in this particular would indeed be inexcusable, now that indulgences applicable to the holy souls are so numerous and so within everyone's power to gain. Yes, it depends on you to come to the relief of your suffering brethren, and it will cost you so little. If you are fortunate enough to gain a plenary indulgence, the soul to which you apply it will probably be freed from the debt it owed, heaven will open to receive it, and, radiant with happiness, it will, at the feet of our Lord, show its everlasting gratitude for its deliverer. "My son," wrote St. Louis at the end of his will, "my last recommendation to you is, that you remember to gain the indulgences of the Church."

EXAMPLE

A Religious, of the Order of St. Francis, concluded an eloquent sermon on almsgiving, by granting his hearers an indulgence of ten days, having received the necessary faculties for so doing. A lady of rank who had been present at the sermon, and who found herself reduced to great penury, came to tell him secretly of her poverty. The good father made her the same answer as did St. Peter to the lame man of Jerusalem, "*Silver and gold I have none, but what I have I give thee* (Acts, 3:6). I renew the assurance I have already given, that you have gained ten days indulgence by being present this morning at my sermon." Naming a banker, he said to her, "Go to him, he is a man who, until now, has never cared for spiritual treasures, but offer to him in return for the alms he will bestow on you, the merit you have gained, so that the sufferings which await him in Purgatory may be lessened. I have good reason to believe that he will give you some help."

The poor lady went as she had been told, and God moved the banker to receive her with kindness. He asked her how much she thought she would get in exchange for her ten days indulgence. "As much," she replied, "as they will weigh in the scales."

"Well," said the banker, "there are the scales: write your ten days on a slip of paper and put it on them. I will put a coin on the other side." Wonderful to relate, the scale did not rise, but outweighed the one with the money. The banker, surprised at the circumstance, added another coin with the same result; then he placed five, ten, thirty, up to a hundred, which was the sum the poor lady needed, and not before this did the scales balance.

It was a lesson for the banker, as until then, he had not known the value of spiritual alms. The poor souls, however, know it still better, and would give all the gold in the world for the smallest indulgence. Let us, then, endeavor to gain for them the greatest number that we possibly can.

PRAYER

O Jesus, Thou knowest my poverty, but, in Thy great mercy, Thou willest that I should find in the treasury of Thy merits and satisfactions the means of supplying for all that is wanting to me. Each day will I come and draw from this ever open treasury the precious indulgences which will pay the debts of my deceased brethren. O Jesus, be merciful to them. May they rest in peace.—*Requiescant in pace.*

TWENTY-SEVENTH DAY

IN WHAT WAY WE CAN AVOID PURGATORY

I. By often thinking of Purgatory.
II. By praying often for the souls in Purgatory.

First Point.—Consider that the thought of Purgatory naturally leads our mind to that of death and judgment, and these cannot fail to inspire us with salutary reflections. "*Remember thy last end,*" says the Holy Spirit, "*and thou shalt never sin*" (Eccl. 7:40). The thought of Purgatory has another advantage, and that is to animate us with a spirit of penance and mortification. At the sight of the dark prison, of the heavy chains, of the burning flames, of the long and cruel tortures, at the sight of the numberless victims who cry out in anguish, the soul enters into itself and exclaims: "I will settle my accounts which have so long been owing to God; I am determined to profit by the time his mercy still grants for me satisfying his justice: I will pay debts that a little generosity and love will so easily furnish me with the means to do. Yes, I am resolved at any price to avoid the torments of Purgatory. I can do so, I ought to do so, and with a little good will and the help of God's grace I shall succeed in doing so."

Would to God, Christian soul, that we had this truth always before our eyes, for it would then be impossible for us not to become saints, and great saints. The habitual thought of Purgatory would free our lives from a multitude of slight faults, would inspire us to practice the highest virtues, and, at the hour of death, our soul, purified by penance and adorned with merits, would wing its flight to heaven without passing through the flames of Purgatory. Oh, what a triumphant and happy death would not this be! O Purgatory! what sublime lessons do you not teach!

Second Point.—The Fathers and Doctors of the Church are of opinion that those who on earth take a lively interest in the souls in Purgatory will be preserved from its flames, or, at least, will not be long detained there; for, say they, the most infallible mark of predestination is to save souls, since God has promised to do the same good to us as we do to others. Blessed are the merciful, for they shall obtain mercy" (Matt. 5:7). Besides, what may we not hope for from the gratitude of the souls we shall have delivered? Could they show themselves less feeling and less charitable than ourselves? At the hour of our death and judgment they will hasten to us and will remain at our side as our protectors and witnesses in our favor, to see that the balance inclines to the side of mercy. They will baffle the snares of the infernal spirit, they will calm the anger of our Judge by their earnest supplications, and obtain for us the most precious of all graces, that of a holy death. "I never remember," said St. Augustine, "to have read anywhere, that he who frequently prayed for the dead, ever died a bad or even doubtful death."

What surer way is there, O Christian soul, for escaping the pains of Purgatory? Let us, then, follow the counsels of the Gospel: "*Make unto you friends of the mammon of iniquity, that when you shall fall they may receive you unto everlasting dwellings*" (Luke, 16:9). Our deceased brethren are now in want, and if we but help them, they will reach heaven, and soon open its gates to us. Oh yes, let us deliver them from the abyss of Purgatory, and they in return will prevent us from falling into it. It is stated that, at the death of St. Catharine of Cortona, all the souls she had delivered came to accompany her in triumph.

EXAMPLE

It is related of a person well known for her devotion to the souls in Purgatory, and the relief of whom had been the object of her life, that when dying, the devil, fearing to lose her, assaulted her violently, surrounding her by all the powers of hell. The dying woman had struggled long and painfully, when suddenly she saw a crowd of unknown, but very beautiful persons enter the room, who putting the devils to flight, came near the bed, and spoke words of encouragement and heavenly consolation. Transported with joy she asked:

"Who are you who do me so much good?"

"We are," replied her benefactors, "the inhabitants of heaven, who have, by means of the suffrages you offered for us, been admitted into eternal happiness, and through gratitude we come in our turn to help you to cross the threshold of eternity, to deliver you from your anguish, and introduce you to the joys of the Holy City."

At these words a smile lit up the face of the dying woman, her eyes closed, and she slept in the peace of the Lord. When her soul appeared before the Sovereign Judge, it was surrounded by as many advocates and protectors as she had delivered souls from Purgatory, and, with them, she entered triumphantly the realms of bliss. Oh, that one day the same happiness may be ours!

PRAYER

O God, do not permit me to banish, through mistaken feelings, the salutary thought of Purgatory. Engrave it on my heart, so that it may prove a powerful means for preserving myself from Purgatory, and for helping the poor souls who are there imprisoned. Happy should I be, could I put an end to their exile, and open to them the gates of heaven.—*Requiescant in pace.*

TWENTY-EIGHTH DAY

APPARITIONS

I. Does God permit the souls in Purgatory to return to earth?
II. For what reason does He permit it?

First Point.—A friend of St. Augustine asked him, one day, the following question: "What ought one to think of the fact that several persons have appeared, after their deaths, going in and out of their houses as formerly? What ought one to think if, in places where their bodies have been buried, at certain hours of the night noises have been heard?" "I am far from believing," replied the great Doctor of the Church, "that these sorts of apparitions are either frequent or natural to the dead; for if it depended on themselves, no night would pass without my seeing my pious mother, who during her life was never separated from me, and who followed me by land and water to far distant countries. But I am convinced that the Almighty can permit, and sometimes does permit them to appear for some good reason that we should respect." *Per divinam potentiam vivorum rebus intersunt.* And why should not

God permit imploring souls who are dear to us, and who still suffer, to speak to us themselves, to tell us their pains, and entreat our compassion? The Holy Scriptures, the Lives of the Saints, and history, all give evidence of well-authenticated apparitions in all times, in every country, and before all classes of witnesses.

Without doubt, it is necessary, O Christian soul, to be on your guard against the too great credulity of certain persons who are forever fancying that they see apparitions of the dead, taking as a reality the vain phantoms of an imagination excited by grief or painful recollections. At the same time, be careful not to deny the possibility of apparitions, as reason tells us that God can permit them, and experience proves that, on different occasions, He has permitted them. These occasions are rare, but they are possible.

Second Point.—Scripture tells us that Samuel appeared after his death to Saul, addressing severe and well-merited reproaches to him. It would seem that a powerful reason for God's granting this permission to the dead, would be on account of the ingratitude of the living, who forgot them, and are solely occupied in enriching themselves with their spoils, and leave them to suffer indefinitely in Purgatory, without giving a thought for their relief or deliverance. When, then, these poor souls appear to living persons, it is generally under a form or in an attitude which excites pity. Often their faces are sad, and burning flames surround them, they sigh deeply, plaintive. cries are heard, or they utter reproaches. Sometimes they make known their presence by sounds, by extraordinary signs; it is always by something which surprises and awakens in us a remembrance of them, exciting us to pray with more fervor for their deliverance.

Blessed be God for making use of all possible means to remind us of the great duty of charity and gratitude towards our deceased brethren. And blessed also may the holy souls of Purgatory be who break through their prison walls, and return to earth to say to us who forget them so often: Have pity on us! *Miserermini mei!*

EXAMPLE

A young man, belonging to an honorable family, had, although faithful to his religious practices, thought little of helping the souls in purgatory. He seldom or never prayed for his deceased relatives; and not only did he neglect this duty, but he persuaded others to do the same, saying: "Why should we care about the dead. for they are certain to be saved, and they cannot lose or offend God any more." He did not believe in apparitions of the souls in Purgatory, and only turned into ridicule those he heard spoken of. God permitted for his correction that some of these souls should leave their prison, and appear under the most frightful forms to him who was doing them so great an injury. In all sorts of places, and at every hour, did they assault him, uttering distressing cries, appearing under strange forms, and leaving him no rest day or night.

The lesson succeeded, a great change was wrought in the young man, who left the world to enter into the Order of St. Dominic; and becoming a priest, he devoted himself in a special manner to the relief of the souls in Purgatory. He offered so many prayers and Masses for them, and preached so often and so eloquently in their behalf, pleading so earnestly for them, that he obtained the name of the *advocate of the dead*; and this he truly was, for no other could give such convincing reasons for proving that the greatest act of charity in this world, was to pray for the dead. The good Dominican died in the odor of sanctity, and his soul, without doubt, joined in heaven those whom his suffrages had liberated from

Purgatory. Let us endeavor to imitate so great an example of charity.

PRAYER

I believe, O my God, that Thou hast not only the power, but that Thou art so merciful as to make use of extraordinary ways to remind us of the suffering members of the Church, and of the assistance they require, making known to us, by these means, how much Thou dost desire that we should help them. O Jesus! be merciful to them; call thy children and our brethren to eternal repose, and may perpetual light shine on them. May they rest in peace.—*Requiescant in pace.*

TWENTY-NINTH DAY

THE LAST WISHES OF THE DEAD

I. We must fulfill them faithfully.
II. We must fulfill them speedily.

First Point.—If there is anything of obligation in this world it is the last wishes of the dying, which should be considered as sacred. The Council of Trent recommends bishops to watch carefully over legacies left by the dead for pious objects, and to see that their wishes are carried out. Other Councils go so far as to excommunicate those who appropriate to themselves the gifts of the dying, or who delay carrying out their last wishes. The severity of these laws shows clearly how guilty those are who deprive the dead of the suffrages they had wished to secure to themselves after their deaths. Woe to those who grow rich on the substance of the poor souls in Purgatory. They deprive them of the relief they would have received, and in a manner constitute themselves their executioners, and, before God, become responsible for their sufferings. But, if the world absolves them for their sacrilegious theft, if it does not stigmatize them with its contempt,

God will not absolve them so easily, and they had better understand that the day will come when He will demand a strict account of these unjust acts, with which they never think of reproaching themselves. They will probably be punished, even in this world, by temporal chastisements; and who can tell us the length and severity of the sufferings that they will have to endure in the next?

Christian soul, reflect seriously; did not your relatives, your friends, your benefactors, when dying, make you some pious recommendation? Did they not ask you either by word of mouth, or in their wills, for prayers, for Masses, or for alms? Did they not, at least, beg you, with tears, to think of them before God? Have you justified the confidence they placed in you, have you fulfilled entirely and conscientiously all the obligations they imposed upon you? If you have not done so, oh, hasten to discharge this sacred debt of justice!

Second Point.—Not only must we execute faithfully the last wishes of the dead, but we must do so as soon as possible, in order not to deprive these dear souls of the relief that would be afforded them, either by Masses celebrated for them, or by the suffrages of the poor, as we should always ask them to pray for their benefactors, when we distribute the alms appointed for them. Every day of delay is a fault for which we are responsible, and which adds to the sufferings of the dead. Did we but understand what these terrible tortures of Purgatory are! Far from putting off the accomplishment of what tends to soften them, we should hasten to bring speedy and efficacious help to these blessed souls who are so worthy of our compassion, and many of whom are so dear to each of us. Alas! how many dishonest heirs have weighty reproaches to make themselves on account of their negligence in fulfilling the sacred engagements they had contracted towards their deceased brethren!

Christian soul, be very careful, and give only to persons worthy of confidence the office of carrying out your last wishes. Place in very safe hands the money destined for good works or Masses for the deliverance of your soul after death. This is the only way of being certain that your last wishes will be carried out, unless it so happens that you have the happiness to belong to one of those Catholic and Christian families who cherish the respect due to the remembrance of the dead.

EXAMPLE

The following incident is an illustration of the punishments which befall those who do not execute the last wishes of the dying. It is related in the chronicles of Charlemagne, that a captain, renowned for his courage, sent, when on his deathbed, for a relative whom he had often benefitted, and turning to him said:

"I have passed sixty years in the service of my king without receiving more than my ordinary pay, and, now that I am dying, I find myself possessed of nothing beyond my faithful horse, which has been so useful to me. When I shall be no more, you must sell my horse and give the price of it to the poor, for the relief of my soul."

The relative promised to do as he wished, but, after the death of the captain, instead of selling the horse, he kept it for himself and never gave any alms to the poor. Hardly had a year elapsed, when the soul of the deceased appeared to his relative, and, addressing him, said:

"Unhappy wretch, you have not executed my last wishes, you have not kept your promise; and you have been the cause of all the sufferings I have endured, from which my alms would have saved me. Know that a speedy death will be your punishment, and, moreover, that a special chastisement is reserved for you. You will not only have to pay the penalty due for your own sins, but you will have to suffer all that I should otherwise have had to suffer, to fully satisfy Divine Justice."

The guilty man, awe-stricken by this threat, and wishing to regulate his conscience, hastened to execute the last wishes of the deceased captain, and do all in his power to escape eternal death; but he could not avoid the death of the body which had been foretold, and which event took place a few days after. How hateful to God is injustice and ingratitude to the dead, which He punishes both in this world and the next.

PRAYER

Grant, O God, that neither cupidity nor culpable negligence, may ever prevent my fulfilling the duties I owe the dead. Their rights are sacred, and their last wishes shall be equally so to me. I will carefully fulfill all the obligations they required of me, and too happy shall I be if, by my promptness and my prayers. I hasten the hour of their deliverance. O Jesus, O Mary, Queen of Purgatory! be merciful to them, and may they rest in heavenly peace! *Requiescant in pace.*

THIRTIETH DAY

PRACTICAL ADVICE

Before concluding the pious exercises of this blessed month, it will be as well, O Christian soul, to reflect on some simple practical truths.

Firstly.—As regards gratitude, rely much on that of the dead, for the dead, said St. Francis of Sales, are always grateful for what has been done for them in this life; but reckon little, very little, on that of the living, and more especially if they are your own children. Your heirs will probably give you a grand funeral and a handsome tombstone, in all of which vanity will have a larger share than either filial or religious affection; and in proportion as they will have been lavish in these things, they will give less to the Church for any of her services. Your heirs will, in all probability, be more eager to quarrel over their inheritance, than to execute your last wishes and free you from Purgatory. Do you not know that, when a person is out of sight, their friends soon lose all recollection of them? As the saying is, "Out of sight, out of mind."

Are you not aware that forgetfulness of the dead is almost universal in these days—*the remembrance of them ends often with the sound of the funeral bell.* And do you not also know that, in what regards your salvation, you must trust to no one but only to yourself? Profit then by the salutary advice given by the author of the *Imitation*, "Trust not in thy friends and kinsfolk, nor put off the welfare of thy soul to hereafter: for men will sooner forget then than thou imaginest. If thou art not now careful for thyself, who will be careful for thee hereafter?" (Imit., 1, 23, 5.)

Secondly.—If you have worldly goods to dispose of, make your will as soon as you can, and do not put it off to your last hour. Who knows, O Christian soul, if your death may not be sudden and unprovided. Experience endorses this advice, for it is well known that many die without having time to make their wills, and before they could arrange what they wished regarding the disposal of their property. "I beg of you," said St. Augustine, "that, before sickness disables you, you will make your will, and put in order the affairs of your household, for, if you wait till you are on your deathbed, menaces and flattery will be made use of to force you to do what you had no intention of doing."

Thirdly.—It is advisable, if you have it in your power, to leave something for religious and charitable works, but more especially make provision for securing to yourself *spiritual assistance*, leaving an alms for anniversary Masses for yourself and your family. He who intends to undertake a long journey to a far-off country makes his preparations in accordance; and will you undertake the long journey from time to eternity, without "taking with you good works to propitiate the Sovereign Judge, and to open for you the Gates of Heaven?   Let the money which you may have, and which is so often made use of for sin and vanity, become a friend to your soul in its affliction. All honor and glory be to our Lord Jesus Christ in this world where we combat, in Purgatory where we suffer, and in Heaven where all will meet again and be united in eternal happiness.

EXAMPLE

A man had three friends, and two of these he loved very particularly. One day he was accused of a great crime of which he was innocent, and turning to his friends he said: "Who will come with me to the court and give testimony to my innocence?"

The first made an excuse alleging that business prevented him; the second accompanied him to the entrance of the court, and turned back, fearing to face the Judge; the third, he on whose friendship the accused reckoned the least, accompanied him, spoke in his favor and testified to his innocence in so convincing a manner that the judge not only liberated him but granted him further privileges.

In this world a man has three friends, and when God, at the hour of death, summons him to judgment, money, his favorite friend, does not accompany him, but leaves him, being no longer of any use to him. His relatives and friends follow him to the grave, sprinkle holy water on his coffin, bid a last farewell, and return quietly to their homes. The third friend, the one he had probably thought the least about during life, are his good works. They, and they only, do not leave him—they accompany him before his Judge, they stand before him, speak in his favor, and obtain mercy and pardon for him: *Opera illorum sequuntur illos.*

Christian soul, when you make your will, leave something for good works, and you will then secure for yourself true friends who will close the gates of Purgatory and open for you those of Heaven. *Hoc fac et vives!*

THE HEROIC ACT

Father Gaspar Oliden, a Theatine Monk, established under the Pontificate of Benedict XIII the devotion entitled the Heroic Act, though, some centuries previous, it appears to have been known in the Church. By a brief, dated August 23rd, 1728, Benedict XIII enriched it with many indulgences, which have been confirmed by Pius VI. and Pius IX. The Heroic Act consists in a voluntary offering made in favor of the faithful departed by any one of the faithful on earth, of all works of satisfaction done by him in this life, as well as of all suffrages which shall be offered for him after death, leaving them all in the hands of the Blessed Virgin to distribute them as she pleases. This heroic act of charity has frequently received the authoritative approbation of the Church. It has also been enriched with great indulgences; but in the course of time doubts have arisen as to some of the conditions for gaining the indulgences, and recently the Sacred Congregation of Indulgences has issued a decree solving five of those most frequently recurring.

The decree decides in the first place, that indulgences declared by the Holy See to be "applicable to the souls in Purgatory," are included amongst the *opera satisfactoria*, which by the Heroic Act are offered for the faithful departed.

Secondly, those who reserve to themselves indulgences granted to the living do not satisfy the conditions, but are bound to apply them all to the holy souls, in accordance with the words of the indult.

Thirdly, it is not an integral part of the Heroic Act that the dispensation of these spiritual favors should be placed in the hands of our Lady. Fourthly, the plenary indulgence which a person who has made the Heroic Act, will gain by going to Holy Communion, or by hearing Mass on Mondays, need not be placed at the disposal of the Blessed Virgin, but may be applied to any of the poor souls at the discretion of the donor. Lastly, a priest who has made the Heroic Act, and who is using the privilege which some priests possess at Mass of what is called a "Privileged Altar," must apply the plenary indulgence gained thereby to the soul of the person for whom the Mass is offered.

This solemn promise does not oblige under pain of sin, and it can be revoked.

ROSARY FOR THE DEAD

On the Cross.

DE PROFUNDIS
(Ps. 129/130)

De profundis clamavi ad te, Domine; *

Domine, exaudi vocem meam.
Fiant aures tuæ intendentes * in vocem deprecationis meæ.
Si iniquitates observaveris, Domine,*
Domine, quis sustinebit?
Quia apud te propitiatio est; *
et propter legem tuam sustinui te, Domine.
Sustinuit anima mea in verbo ejus: *
speravit anima mea in Domino.
A custodia matutina

Out of the depths I have cried to thee, O Lord:
Lord, hear my voice.

Let thy ears be attentive to the voice of my supplication.
If thou, O Lord, wilt mark iniquities: Lord, who shall stand it.
For with thee there is merciful forgiveness: and by reason of thy law, I have waited for thee, O Lord. My soul hath relied on his word:
my soul hath hoped in the Lord.
From the morning

usque ad noctem, *
speret Israël in
Domino.
Quia apud Dominum
misericordia, *
et copiosa apud eum
redemptio.
Et ipse redimet Israël *
ex omnibus
iniquitatibus ejus.

watch even until night,
let Israel hope in the
Lord.
Because with the Lord
there is mercy: and
with him plentiful
redemption.
And he shall redeem
Israel from all his
iniquities.

PATER NOSTER

Pater noster, qui es in
caelis, sanctificetur
nomen tuum. Adveniat
regnum tuum. Fiat
voluntas tua, sicut in
caelo et in terra.
Panem nostrum
quotidianum da nobis
hodie, et dimitte nobis
debita nostra sicut et
nos dimittimus
debitoribus nostris. Et
ne nos inducas in
tentationem, sed libera
nos a malo. Amen.

Our Father, who art in
heaven, hallowed be
Thy name. Thy
kingdom come. Thy
will be done on earth
as it is in heaven.
Give us this day our
daily bread and forgive
us our trespasses as we
forgive those who
trespass against us.
And lead us not into
temptation, but deliver
us from evil. Amen.

AVE MARIA

Ave Maria, gratia plena, Dominus tecum. Benedicta tu in mulieribus, et benedictus fructus ventris tui, Jesus. Sancta Maria, Mater Dei, ora pro nobis peccatoribus, nunc, et in hora mortis nostrae. Amen.

Hail Mary, full of grace, the Lord is with thee. Blessed art thou amongst women and blessed is the fruit of thy womb, Jesus. Holy Mary, Mother of God, pray for us sinners, now, and in the hour of our death. Amen.

On the Large Beads.

Requiem aeternum, dona eis Domine, et lux perpetua, luceat eis.

Eternal rest grant to them, O Lord, and let perpetual light shine upon them.

ACT OF FAITH

My God, I believe in Thee, because Thou art Truth itself.

ACT OF HOPE

I hope in Thee, because Thou art infinitely good.

ACT OF CHARITY

I love Thee with my whole heart, and above all things, because Thou art infinitely perfect, and I love my neighbor as myself for the love of Thee.

On the Small Beads.

Sweet Heart of Mary, be my salvation.
(To conclude with a Pater and Ave.)

The forty small beads of which the Rosary is composed are in honor of the forty hours our Blessed Lord spent in the sepulcher.

Twenty-three thousand, three hundred days' indulgence may be gained each time it is repeated.

The devotion may be performed with or without particular beads. No special blessing is required for the Rosary.